How to Talk
with Your Child
About Sexuality

How to Talk with Your Child About Sexuality

Planned Parenthood®
FAYE WATTLETON, *President*
with ELISABETH KEIFFER

Doubleday & Company, Inc., Garden City, New York, 1986

Library of Congress Cataloging-in-Publication Data

How to talk with your child about sexuality.

Bibliography: p. 188
Includes index.
1. Sex instruction for children.   2. Parent and child.   I. Wattleton,
Faye.   II. Keiffer, Elisabeth.   III. Planned Parenthood® Federation of Amer-
ica.
HQ57.H675 1986   649'.65   85-30767
ISBN 0-385-18443-3
ISBN 0-385-18444-1 (pbk.)

Contents

Introduction   ix

Part I: What Is Involved in Sexuality Teaching   1

CHAPTER 1:   Talking About Sex and Sexuality
Children Learn Most About Sexuality At Home   3
Why Sexuality Is So Hard To Talk About   5
It Is Much More Than "The Talk"   10

CHAPTER 2:   "How Do I Start?"
The Earlier You Start, The Easier It Is   15
Boys Should Be Included   19
When Children Learn From Parents, Everyone Benefits   21

CHAPTER 3:   "What Should I Do?"
Answering Questions   24
Listening, Hearing—and More Listening   26
Privacy: Everyone Needs It   29

CHAPTER 4:   Growing Up with Self-Esteem   33

CHAPTER 5:   Letting Children Know It Is Safe to Be Sexual   37

Part II: The Facts   45

CHAPTER 6:   What They Want to Know—Preschoolers to
High Schoolers   47
The Preschooler   49
The Early Grade School Years (Ages Six to Nine)   51
The Preteen Years (Ages Nine to Twelve)   56

CHAPTER 7:   The Top Seven Questions   61
Menstruation   61
The Big Changes for Boys   69
Masturbation   73
Intercourse and Pregnancy   77
Birth Control   81
Sexually Transmissible Diseases (STDs)   87
Homosexuality   90

CHAPTER 8:   Talking About Values   94

Part III: Help in Special Situations   107

CHAPTER 9:   Facing Facts   109
And Dealing With Consequences   112

CHAPTER 10:   Protecting Children From Sexual Abuse   125
What Parents Should Know About Child Molestation   125
How to Prevent Child Abuse   127
When a Child Has Been Abused   131
Dealing With the Possibility of a Daughter's Rape   133

CHAPTER 11:   Sex and the Single Parent   138

CHAPTER 12:   Sex and the Latchkey Child   146

Afterword   151

Appendices: 153

A Glossary of Sexual Terms   155

Facts About Methods of Contraception 170

Facts About STDs 182

Selected Bibliography for Parents and Children 188

Index 195

Introduction

Planned Parenthood celebrates its seventieth anniversary in 1986. For decades, millions of parents across the country have turned to Planned Parenthood educators for advice about when/whether/why/how they should talk with their children about sexuality, puberty, contraception, and pregnancy. This book, written for parents and their children of all ages, provides information validated over the years as well as suggested responses to their most frequently asked questions.

The need for parents to talk with their children about these sensitive subjects has never been greater. In today's society, we are all bombarded with sexual messages everywhere we turn—from the mass media to the locker-room walls. Often these messages are unrealistic; at worst they completely misrepresent the facts.

We all are vulnerable to the pressures and distortions of these messages, and our children are not exempt. Indeed they are more susceptible than the rest of us because we do not prepare them with sound sexual information. Only 10 percent of students nationwide receive what can be considered comprehensive, timely sexuality education in their classrooms. In the home, while more parents than ever are talking with their children about sex, many of the most sensitive areas of sexuality are omitted from the conversations.

As a result, most of our children are uninformed or misinformed. They are ill-equipped to face the complexities of sexual maturation. Young people are confused, frightened, and bursting with unanswered, often unasked questions. The consequences are staggering. More than one million teenage girls in this country become pregnant every year—a growing human tragedy unmatched in all other developed nations.

Planned Parenthood believes that information and education are keys to helping our children grow up knowledgeable and capable of making informed choices—about sexuality, as well as about other important aspects of their lives. And we believe that parents are and should be the primary sexuality educators of their children—providing the accurate information their children want and need, from the time they are born.

This book is designed to help parents in that role. It was written with the invaluable assistance of many people in the Planned Parenthood family, a network of 187 affiliates that serve parents and their children in more than 700 communities nationwide. We hope you will benefit from our insights, just as we have benefitted from the opportunity to develop this book. As in all creative undertakings, we gained more than we gave. We learned not only to better understand the process of parenting but, most importantly, that there is always more to learn.

This book is dedicated to parents and to their responsibilities as the first and most effective teachers of their children. Finally it is dedicated to our children. The future belongs to them, and it is up to us to see they are strong enough and wise enough to make the best use of their inheritance.

FAYE WATTLETON

How to Talk
with Your Child
About Sexuality

PART I

What Is Involved in Sexuality Teaching

CHAPTER 1

Talking About Sex and Sexuality

CHILDREN LEARN MOST ABOUT SEXUALITY AT HOME

The changes in sexual attitudes, behavior, and lifestyles that have taken place in our society over the past twenty-five years present today's parents—and children—with some of the most complex issues they will ever confront.

As soon as children are able to look, listen, and comprehend, they can't avoid the messages about sex that permeate life today. It is used to sell products and entertainment; it makes headlines in the newspapers; it is, most explicitly, the subject of popular songs. Many parents are concerned about the impact these messages have and wonder whether such messages present boys and girls with pressures they aren't ready for and may erect barriers to their growing up to be healthy, successful adults.

They have good reason to worry. Consider just these few facts:

· Over one million teenage girls in the United States get pregnant every year, more than 80 percent of them unintentionally.

- In 1982 there were two million new cases of sexually transmitted diseases among people under twenty-five.
- As few as 10 percent of high school girls who become unmarried mothers finish school.
- More than half of teenage marriages end in divorce.
- Despite the overwhelming 90 percent approval of parents, only New Jersey, Maryland, and the District of Columbia mandate sexuality education in schools. Fewer than 15 percent of all big-city schools offer timely, comprehensive sexuality education.

What these statistics say is that the prevailing lack of information and understanding about human sexuality in this country is putting many young people in danger—of confusion, unhappiness, disease, and economic hardship.

Before we go any farther, let us define what we mean by "sexuality." It is far more than that mysterious entity used to sell everything from blue jeans to automobiles, far more than the physical act of intercourse. Sexuality is part of the makeup and personality of every human being. It lets us know which gender we belong to. It can define our role in society and influence our feelings about our relationships with others. It makes it possible for us to feel love, compassion, joy, and sorrow. Our sexuality basically determines the way we lead our everyday lives. We have to understand its role if we expect to understand ourselves or why we behave as we do.

That concept, one our grandparents never heard of, is neither easy to learn nor easy to teach, but it is central to all of us throughout our lives.

It is only natural to want our children to grow up with healthy bodies and minds, to want to equip them to get the best out of life in terms of lasting friendships and committed, loving relationships, to want to instill values and attitudes that will serve them well when they are on their own. An understanding of human sexuality is involved in all these things, and that is what makes our task as parents so difficult. For a number of reasons, talking about sexual matters with our own children is difficult for almost everyone.

Whether parents realize it or not, one of the most important sources, and for most children the first source, of learning about sexuality is the home. This book is written with the hope that we at Planned Parenthood can help parents make it the best source.

Ensuring that children grow up to be adults capable of making healthy decisions about their sexuality calls for a parent-child dialogue that should begin much earlier than most parents would expect. Sexual learning is a lifelong process; sexual teaching begins for parents at the birth of their first child and, when it is most successful, continues to unfold as the child's needs grow and change.

Guiding a child's development and answering questions about sexual matters honestly and without embarrassment is not easy for many parents. We hope this book will make parents more comfortable with the process. And we hope it will do even more. The parents who are most successful at maintaining a relaxed and mutually trusting dialogue with their children through the years are those who have learned to do more than deal with questions as they arise. They are mothers and fathers who take the initiative instead of waiting until children ask, who use opportunities in everyday life to make it clear to children that sexual matters are a normal part of our lives and can be talked about comfortably. If reading this book helps parents develop that skill, we will have accomplished our goal.

WHY SEXUALITY IS SO HARD TO TALK ABOUT

Scenes very like the one that follows are being played out across the country as increasing numbers of parents grapple with their concern over the kind of sexual learning that takes place in our society.

Nearly thirty adults, strangers to one another, sit around a table in the cafeteria of a small-town community center. Most of them are women; six have their husbands with them, and one divorced man is there alone. What do these men and women have in common? Only the fact that they are parents who share the same need. Every person in the room has a child or children aged from seven up into the teens. All of them recognize that whether they welcome the role or not, they are their children's primary teachers about sexuality. And they are not at all sure of how to handle it. And so they have paid the fee for a series of group discussions with a professional sex educator.

The divorced father puts it this way: "I want to help my kids deal with the double message they are getting every day. On the one hand, they're supposed to believe sex is a no-no. On the other, they're pressured into it from every side."

"I don't want my girls to make the same mistakes I did," a young woman says forthrightly. "I'm twenty-nine, and I've been divorced twice. I was fifteen the first time I got married. I got pregnant just to get away from home."

"Our fourteen-year-old son tells his father and me our values are totally passé," another mother volunteers. "Since he considers every question from us an invasion of his privacy, we can't find out what *his* values are."

"What is it you want to get across to your kids?" asks the sex educator. "Would you write down on the cards in front of you three messages you would like to give your children?"

That turns out to be simple. In an astonishingly short time, both sides of every card are filled. And when they are gathered up and the messages are read aloud, they turn out to be so straightforward, so sensible, and so loving that one might wonder why these particular parents need help in communicating with their children.

But they do.

We all do, it seems. And that is not so surprising. Human sexuality is perhaps the most personal—and vulnerable—characteristic we share. Talking about sexuality raises questions literally or by implication about ourselves and our sex lives, questions that we don't enjoy discussing. Nevertheless these parents, like many others, want to try because they know that giving their children a realistic perspective on sexuality is as important as giving them food, shelter, and loving care.

"What messages did you get from your parents about sex?" is the next question put to the group.

"It was never mentioned."

"I didn't get any information at all."

"They said not to do it."

"I got the idea it was something dirty."

"My mother told me boys were just after one thing."

These parents are amazed to learn how similar their childhood experiences have been. But, in fact, it is likely that every adult can recall some variation on the same theme. Sex was often a taboo subject when our parents were raising families because it was generally associated narrowly with the sex act itself. And that was considered inappropriate for "innocent" children to know about. So it was referred to guardedly or not discussed in front of—or with—children at all. But children are adept at learning from what is unsaid as well as what is said. They pick up cues from facial expressions, gestures—and silence. The message we heard when we were children was extremely powerful: Sex is supposed to be a secret, so it must be something really bad.

Long after we grew up and made our own discoveries about sexuality—which often revealed that our parents had not been entirely candid—the old taboo remained. Though parents of children these days may have themselves been teens during the 1960s "sexual revolution," they learned how to be parents from their parents, who were probably teens in the 1930s or '40s—not very open times. Attitudes may be changing, but it's a slow process.

"It's like my parents' attitudes have a way of rising up from some subconscious level to sabotage me when I try to talk to my children about it," a young mother comments.

She's not alone in that feeling. Most of us possess a great many attitudes and beliefs that we have carried over from childhood and still follow, whether they are useful any longer or not. Such messages as "That's the way Mother always fixed it" or "That's how Dad said it was" remain incredibly potent. And attitudes and beliefs about sexuality are probably as deeply ingrained as any.

It is worth thinking about these attitudes and deciding where —or even if—they fit today, not only for our own sakes but for our children's. If we can learn to deal more openly, honestly, comfortably with our youngsters, the chances are that they will not only grow up happier but may turn out to be better sexuality teachers of *their* children.

"I think what makes it hardest to talk to our kids is the double standard involved," says one of the fathers present. "How can you help but feel like a hypocrite when what you're trying to put across is that it's okay for me and other adults to have sexual feelings, but it's not okay for kids to."

Indeed, emotionally most of us find it so far from all right that we try to forget that all children, even as infants, are sexual beings. Because this biological-psychological fact seems incompatible with the innocence society has always ascribed to children, it strikes adults as perplexing. Because it suggests the possibility that if children have sexual feelings they may decide to act them out, it is also regarded as threatening.

Both adults and children are victims of the biological and economic changes that have taken place over the past century. Thanks to good food and health care, the average age at which girls today have their first menstrual period is several years younger than that of their grandmothers—around twelve and a half instead of sixteen (the age at which our grandmothers often married). Boys are also capable of fathering children at a younger age than their forebears. So, worrisomely to adults, it has all gotten out of sync. Boys and girls are physiologically ready for sexual activity before the society they live in makes it possible for them to cope with its emotional, physical, and economic consequences.

But how do you explain that to *them?* It certainly isn't easy.

Every mother and father can contribute other reasons for finding sexual matters hard to discuss with their own children.

"I always have the feeling they'll think I'm talking about what my husband and I do, and that makes me feel weird," a mother says.

We all feel a little "weird" under these circumstances because we remember how difficult it is for children to think of their parents as sexual beings. It is bound to make us feel self-conscious.

"I really don't know what my daughter wants to know, and so I don't know where to begin."

This mother is worrying, as a great many do, that if she gives her child information prematurely, she'll stimulate a preoccupation with sex. Our long experience with young people at Planned Parenthood has taught us that this simply does not happen. However, we have seen repeatedly that misunderstanding, misinformation, or no information can confuse and frighten youngsters and lead to the very vulnerability parents fear most. The young person, refused information from a reliable source, may go elsewhere and obtain misinformation.

Another mother is concerned that her children already know as much about the subject as she does and feels she will look foolish if she volunteers information which may not be completely accurate. What she might do from time to time is to check their level of knowledge. Like any other teaching situation, it is useful to determine how much the student already knows before providing information. What is happening in the family, the neighborhood, even the world can provide conversational openers.

"What worried us is that neither of our boys has ever asked us a single question. We don't know how to break the ice," one member of a couple says.

Often without consciously meaning to or even being aware they are doing it, adults create an atmosphere that discourages any questions about sexual matters. Children are quick to read nonverbal messages like facial expressions, tones of voice, changes of subject, or obvious uneasiness. This happens so often it provides reason enough for parents to initiate—not to wait to be asked—a dialogue about sexual subjects as early as possible, before the child is old enough to be aware that his or her questions cause adults discomfort.

IT IS MUCH MORE THAN "THE TALK"

It used to be called "telling them about the facts of life." The mental picture that phrase conjures up is of an embarrassed parent sitting down with a son or daughter and running through a hasty review of the anatomical differences between males and females and an even hastier description of how the human race reproduces.

Then some of our schools began teaching it and it was called "sex education." A lot of parents breathed a sigh of relief, figuring they were off the hook. That, however, is not quite the case. Sex education in elementary school, when it happens at all, involves five hours or less of teaching time in a year. At the junior and senior high school levels, it most often consists of six to ten hours of teaching time over an entire year and typically covers anatomy, physiology, family roles and relationships, and (sometimes) contraception.

Other parents don't like the idea of sex education courses for a variety of reasons. Some fear their children will adopt values incompatible with theirs. Others believe that all these classes accomplish is to acquaint children with how to have sex without fear of consequences. While the controversy about sex education in schools continues, the fact remains that there is a lot more to sexuality education than an explanation of the anatomical differences between boys and girls, hygiene, and birth control.

Sexuality education is not just one talk, or even one course taught in school. It is a process that begins, without words, in infancy and continues into adulthood. The scope of the information conveyed changes as children grow, but the essential qualities of successful communication—openness and honesty and caring—do not.

Giving young children the information they need about sexual development is relatively simple. Their questions are usually quite matter of fact and can be answered in that spirit. They dote on facts. Teenagers, on the other hand, would like to ask their parents—yes, their parents—much more complicated questions. They are deeply preoccupied with finding out who they are and what their relationships with other people should be. On the surface these concerns may not always seem as directly related to sexuality as "Where do babies come from?" but in fact they usually are.

The way teenagers handle their feelings and behavior concerning their sexuality depends in large part on how they see themselves. If they have reason to believe they are pretty okay people, if they have been taught since they were little that they deserve respect from other people, they will be much better prepared to make unpressured decisions about what they do. They need all the help they can get when it comes to resisting pressure. Don't underestimate that!

Planned Parenthood of Chicago surveyed one thousand young men and asked them if they felt it was all right to lie to a girl about being in love with her in order to get her to have sex. Seventy percent of them said, "Yes!" If teenagers have learned to respect other people's feelings and bodies and believe they deserve the same treatment, teenagers will be less vulnerable. If they have been taught since early childhood that every act has a consequence, they may see, when the time comes, that this is also true of sexual activity.

And if they have been helped to realize that sex is probably one of the most profound experiences two people can share, they will be on their way to understanding what makes a good relationship.

Explaining "the facts of life" is only the smallest part of one of the most important subjects parents can teach.

This book is written for both parents, even though we realize that traditionally mothers have been the persons to whom children bring their questions. However, today the rigid stereotyping of parental roles is changing. More mothers are working outside the home; more fathers are sharing the age-old women's responsibilities of keeping house and raising the children. In doing so, they are finding that they welcome the greater closeness with their children. In return, their children are seeing them as more emotionally supportive and approachable with questions.

Many families are finding this new structure has a number of benefits. Fathers have always played an important part in teaching their children about sexuality, even if they never discussed any aspect of it with them. Their behavior, their attitudes, their values provide essential models to both male and female children of what masculinity is about. But if information, verbal information, comes only from mothers, the message to boys and girls is unmistakable: "Males do not need to be responsible about sexual matters. Sexuality is strictly a female issue." That is a message we need to erase today.

It used to be assumed that if fathers were going to be instructors at all, they were only responsible for "the Talk"—that mutually embarrassed session—with their sons. The mother's duty was to inform daughters as the need arose. Again this represents a stereotyping of roles and the waste of valuable information resources. Who can help an adolescent girl understand why her boyfriend behaves as he does and how to deal with him better than another male? By the same token, mothers can tell sons plenty about girls. In practical terms, the key may be for the parent with the better relationship with the child to be the educator. That parent has the best chance of being heard. Sometimes an older brother or sister may be the parents' best ally.

A number of studies of sexual learning in American families have shown that while fathers would like to convey their values on the subject of sexuality to their children, they very often subscribe to a much stricter code of behavior for their daughters than they do for their sons. This can lead in many cases to an unspoken mother-daughter—or, sometimes, mother-son—agreement to keep Dad in the dark as much as possible. A mother may say to her shy son, "I understand why you didn't want to ask her to the prom, but your father may not. He really wants you to be more social, but what he doesn't know won't hurt him." Or a mother may say to her popular daughter, "Let's just not tell your dad that you and Jim went together to the city for the weekend. It would just upset him, and he doesn't need to know." To us at Planned Parenthood, this seems an unproductive and divisive way for marriage partners to deal with their children's sexuality. When parents can talk over and agree on their expectations of children's behavior, and can present a united front to them, sexuality education becomes a less formidable task, and all relationships in the family are strengthened.

In many families today there are not two parents at home. About 21 percent of all children under eighteen live with one or no parents. The great majority of such children live with their mothers. One of the questions mothers without husbands at home ask is what effect the absence of a father has on the children.

Lacking a masculine image at home on whom they can model themselves, boys may have difficulty developing an image of what being a man involves. Girls without fathers may also experience problems with gender roles. Mothers can help their sons and daughters by making sure they see a lot of male relatives, family friends, or teachers who can substitute as father images. Boys can be encouraged to join boys' clubs and organizations. Girls can be encouraged to make friends with children of both sexes from the time they are little.

In the final section of this book, we'll devote a chapter to child-rearing problems and their solutions for single parents.

CHAPTER 2

"How Do I Start?"

THE EARLIER YOU START, THE EASIER IT IS

One reason parents find talking to children about sexual matters uncomfortable is that they mistakenly assume the subject has the same emotional significance for the child as it has for them. This is not the case where young children are concerned. The concept of adult sexual behavior—the kind parents are thinking of—is not relevant to them, but they do have great curiosity and they love facts. This is why it is so useful to begin talking with them when they are small, and to answer their questions truthfully.

Is there anything embarrassing about explaining to a three-year-old why the traffic light changes from red to green? A question like "Why does Daddy have a penis and you don't?" is asked in the same spirit. Keeping that in mind should make it possible to talk about anatomical differences and biological facts with greater ease.

Many parents confess that they avoid discussions of sexual topics with their children because they are afraid they won't know the answers to their children's questions, and as a result will feel inadequate. There is nothing wrong with admitting you don't know something. It doesn't, as adults subconsciously fear, make a child think less of you. If you don't know all the answers, don't be afraid to say so. Offer to look for them. Planned Parenthood and other family services agencies offer a variety of literature, much of it free, for just this purpose.

There is also no reason a parent shouldn't admit to feeling uncomfortable, if that is the case, about discussing sexual matters. Talking about illness or bathroom habits makes some people uncomfortable. Crowds make others uneasy. Nobody looks down on them for it. A youngster whose parent says honestly, "This is hard for me to talk about," not only feels sympathy for the parent but has the comforting feeling that the embarrassment filling the room is not coming from *him*. In other words, the subject is okay. The discomfort lies in the parent's personal ability to discuss it.

It is worth mentioning the research finding that children do not usually show embarrassment about discussing pregnancy and childbirth until they are around eight. How much less they might show if, by that age, the concept had gradually become a familiar and comfortable one?

Much of a child's sexual learning takes place gradually, informally, and incidentally. When parents are aware of this, they can take advantage of the countless opportunities in family life to get across the messages they consider important. Gender learning, for instance, begins at a very early age. Identifying oneself as male or female will determine many of one's sexual attitudes, behavior, and values. Children learn this primarily from their parents' attitudes. Affection and expressions of emotion are also learned by observing other adults. When husbands and wives openly show their affection and closeness, children learn that these are safe, comfortable behaviors that represent happiness.

Children also learn about sexuality through their bodies—by discovering what they can do, seeing how they look, experiencing the variety of sensations they are capable of. As they get older, increasing awareness of their parents' attitudes about bathroom etiquette and nudity will expand children's "body learning."

Besides instructing children nonverbally through behavior and attitude, parents can begin to use attitudes as subjects of conversation even with very young children. Naming body parts can be a bathtub game with toddlers; an explanation of the anatomical differences between boys and girls can be offered before it is asked for; affection, as a concept, can be talked about as well as shown.

Following are just a few ways parents can create opportunities to start the long process of sexually educating young children:

- Looking through family albums together provides a very personal introduction to subjects like weddings and childbirth and family relationships. Little children are fascinated by pictures of themselves in earlier years. Parents can point out pictures taken "before you were born."
- Children's books with pictures of people provide a springboard for talking about how these people are behaving toward one another and how they illustrate gender roles. Even more specific and useful are books for young children that deal with reproduction and sexuality.
- A pregnancy or birth in the family or neighborhood is worth pointing out and talking about, even if the child hasn't noticed it.
- Suggesting pictures that little children might draw—a boy, a girl, a mommy and daddy, a baby being born—and then talking about them can alert parents to areas of confusion children may have.
- The behavior of animals in zoos, on a farm, in a park, or at home often provokes questions from children. It's important, though, to make sure they understand that humans have human babies and animals have animal babies. Children take things they are told very literally. A child psychologist tells of a mother who gave the birth of ducklings as an example of

reproduction and was amazed to learn that her daughter interpreted it as meaning that to get a baby one went to a store
and bought a duck!

Television, of course, is the most omnipresent instructor,
both good and bad, of children. Statistics indicate that six-
year-olds watch TV an average of twenty-eight hours a week.
It's worthwhile to watch with them when you can, to ask how
they feel about the scenes and behavior they see, and to let
them, in turn, know how you feel.

If parents have made it a habit to use everyday occasions to
start conversations about sexual matters that may be puzzling
children, by the time children are eight or nine they will have
taken in the basic factual information. This knowledge will
then provide a foundation for a continuing dialogue on the
more complex social, moral, and emotional issues of sexuality.
By this age, a youngster's constantly expanding world will provoke all sorts of questions. But children will be reluctant to ask
such questions now unless a comfortable climate for question-
ing has already been established in the family.

And if they don't ask, society abounds with sexual messages
that parents can use as openers for conversations on such subjects as why people get married, why they have children, what
makes a good marriage, the advantages and disadvantages of
being male or female, and so on. Talking about social behavior
with prepubertal children is not only a useful way to work into
the subject of sexuality, but social behavior is also an important subject in and of itself. It is also easier and more helpful to
discuss these subjects while they are regarded as neutral in a
child's mind. Intercourse and when it is appropriate, why some
teenagers risk pregnancy, sexual myths, and other topics like
these are much more easily talked about in the years before
they become personal issues. It can be useful to remember that
the attitudes parents convey when the issues are not emotionally charged have a far better chance of registering.

We can't say it too often: The earlier parents begin educating their children sexually, the easier it is to do. The parents' answers should be simple and truthful. Let the child direct you—don't tell him or her more than he or she wants to know. But even if it has been put off longer than it should have been, late is definitely better than never.

BOYS SHOULD BE INCLUDED

A male sex therapist, Jay Gale, wrote the following passage:

> When I was growing up, I kept thinking that somehow I was going to learn about sex. My parents never mentioned it and I had no books to learn from, but I thought that magically, as I got older, I would understand the strange things that were happening to my mind and body. . . . I was feeling crazy, driven by all sorts of urges and feelings. I don't think I ever felt so alone. . . . I was sure I was the only person who ever went through such an experience. I needed information but I had no idea where to get it.

Unfortunately his confession is not an unusual one. When fathers are only marginally involved in infant care, they are deprived of some of the joys of parenthood. In the same way, societal attitudes have shortchanged sons as much or more when it comes to learning about human sexuality at home.

The reason is obvious, though incredibly shortsighted. Fear of daughters becoming pregnant is what drives parents to inform girls, at least minimally, about sex. For females, ignorance involves a measurable risk.

But boys are at risk as well. They have just as great a need for honest information, for reassurance about themselves, for learning to understand their roles and responsibilities in relationships with the opposite sex. They are just as likely, if not more likely, than girls to rely dangerously on all kinds of misinformation, since they are each other's principal informants. *They* won't get pregnant, but they can get a girl pregnant, contract a sexually transmitted disease, worry themselves sick, and make someone else miserable.

Our society gives tacit, if not explicit, permission for young men to "sow their wild oats." We, however, encourage both parents to see themselves as responsible for their sons' and daughters' equal education about human sexuality.

We asked a typical group of small-town high school boys, ages fifteen and sixteen, whether they believe *parents* spend as much time explaining sex to sons as they do to daughters. Out of twenty-eight boys, twenty-one said "no," two said "yes," and five said they "don't know." Asked if they would like their fathers to talk to them about sex, only three volunteered that "he already does."

If anyone believes boys don't need reliable information about sexuality fully as much as girls, the next question and answer should dispel the idea. "Is there as much pressure on teenage boys to have sex as there is on girls?" we asked. Of the respondents, sixteen of the twenty-eight boys said "yes," six said "more," and two said they "don't know." Their female classmates agreed. When girls were asked the same question, thirty out of forty said "yes" or "more." Most respondents of both sexes explained that the pressure came from boys.

What do teenage boys want to know about? One of them probably answered for the majority when he wrote, "Everything about sex. Education should start at nursery school and build in sophistication until the eighth grade. At that point, every aspect of bodies should be taught and discussed."

His was the most eloquent plea, but the others were just as touching. Among the things these boys wanted to know were:

How they're different inside.
About their bodies and girls' bodies.
If they're normal.
Why they do or do not have an urge for sex.
When they will start maturing emotionally.

If boys almost ready to leave high school still have questions as fundamental and innocent as these, it is hard to imagine how they can be expected to engage in adult, responsible, caring relationships with other human beings.

WHEN CHILDREN LEARN FROM PARENTS, EVERYONE BENEFITS

As parents we have no choice but to be teachers. We teach our babies to walk and talk. We instruct them in holding a spoon and using the toilet. Earlier than we realize, perhaps, we impart to them feelings about right and wrong, good and bad. Being this powerful gives us a big responsibility, but it also gives us an opportunity no one else has.

"I used to think I'd have trouble explaining sex to my children," a widowed father told us, "until I realized it was kind of a challenge. I saw that I could get to them first and tell it to them straight before anyone else filled their heads with a lot of junk."

That is certainly an opportunity worth grabbing. Today a boy or girl competent enough to turn on a TV set or flip the pages of a magazine is being barraged with messages about sex that must be confusing to a degree that is hard for adults to comprehend. When children's curiosity isn't satisfied about why or how something happens, they are likely to make up their own explanations. That is why they have always exchanged such fables as "You had one but it fell off" or "Babies have to come out of your belly button—why else would it be there?"

Sometimes the misinformation young people passed back and forth through the ages was upsetting or frightening, but it had nothing like the potential for confusion and fear of the messages children constantly receive today.

With the complexity of today's world, it really does pay to start to provide your children with adequate information. Even though the parental role of teacher can pall at times—as in toilet training or teaching table manners—it is a vital part of the bond between parents and their children. As parents we really want the offspring we love to learn from us the things that matter most. Otherwise why would we feel that twinge of jealousy when other influences begin entering their lives?

As they grow and mature, there will be many instances in which having been given a sound perspective about sexuality from an early age will prove invaluable to your children. Almost inevitably, they are going to be exposed to a full array of sexual messages. Explicit sexual material can turn up without warning on the TV screens, in daily conversations with their friends, or on public newsstands. Unlike books or magazines, the contents of television shows cannot always be anticipated, and the impact of seeing live actors is definitely greater than looking at still photos.

However, most sex educators believe that the effect on young viewers is considerably less disturbing if they have already been given an honest understanding of sexual relations. Children who understand how the depiction of people having intercourse fits into the overall fabric of sexuality find it much less fascinating—or frightening—than those who lack any perspective on it.

Another important reason to educate children early is that sexual abuse of children is terrifyingly widespread, as society is belatedly beginning to recognize. (We will talk about ways to arm children against such abuse in a later chapter.) To warn children effectively and noninjuriously, we have to help them understand the difference between what is positive and healthy and what is not.

When boys and girls reach adolescence, the benefits of having educated them early are even more apparent. This is the age when sexually maturing teens are particularly vulnerable to peer pressure and most accepting of peer misinformation. There seem to be so many urgent reasons to respond to their emotions, to do what they believe everyone else their age is doing, that other alternatives are not always considered.

Understanding the consequences of sexual activity and recognizing the need for being responsible are vital now. Misinformation or lack of information can only produce disillusionment and unhappiness. The teenager who believes she can't get pregnant if she has intercourse standing up really exists. There are thousands like her.

Planned Parenthood and other family service agencies deal with the disastrous consequences of this kind of ignorance all the time.

A number of studies have shown that adolescent girls who have been given an honest and sound education in human sexuality become unintentionally pregnant much less often than girls who have not, and they are also likely to postpone sexual relations longer than their uninformed sisters.

Parents will never be their children's only educators, even if they want to be. They would have to keep them locked away from every outside influence to accomplish that. But parents can be, and more than ever in history need to be, their children's first and most important teachers. Consider how often your child asks you, "Is it true that . . . ?" about *anything*. They want to be able to ask their parents about sex in that same way.

CHAPTER 3

"What Should I Do?"

ANSWERING QUESTIONS

When teenagers are polled as to where they would prefer to get information about sex—from friends, counselors in school, or from their parents—nine out of ten say "from parents." That's the good news. The bad news is that the number who actually go to their parents for information is more like *one* out of ten. The reason most of them give is that their parents are reluctant to talk.

"If I ask her anything, she tells me, 'Later.' She doesn't like to talk about it," is a typical teenage comment.

Parental willingness to talk is certainly the first requirement, but it takes more than that to open the lines of communication about sexuality with a child and, equally important, to keep them open throughout the stormy, perilous years of adolescence. What is it that makes some parents more successful than others in keeping an easy flow of communication going with their children? Where there is open affection, mutual trust, and a willingness on the part of adults to admit their own frailties, there is usually good communication. In addition, a base of accurate information is necessary as well as skills in sharing that information, skills that are not too hard to perfect.

One way to establish a firm basis for continuing communication is to be a good "question answerer" from the very beginning. Asking questions is how three- and four-year-olds learn. They ask a lot of them about everything, and their timing is often horrendous. But in that intimate interplay of question and answer there is a lot more involved than the subject matter or timing. The child is saying, "I trust you," and the way the parent replies tells the child either "I care enough about you to take the trouble to answer your question" or "Your question is annoying, silly, or displeasing to me."

Children discover very quickly whether their parents consider them important and are rewarding people to ask questions of. A parent who is "askable" answers clearly, honestly, and patiently and is willing to answer the same question as many times as necessary for the child to understand. Such parents neither ridicule nor ignore their children's questions.

When young children don't ask questions about sex, it doesn't mean they aren't curious. Rather it means they have somehow formed the impression that sex is a subject that will be greeted with displeasure or discomfort. To avoid the displeasure they satisfy their curiosity somewhere else, probably with misinformation.

Nobody, of any age, likes to be laughed at. But the literal-mindedness of small children frequently prompts them to ask questions that seem pretty funny to adults. It is hard for any parent to keep a serious expression when confronted with "But how does he take his penis off to put it in the lady's vagina?" However, it's important to try. The little boy is serious, even though the mental image he conjures up may be comical.

Children ask questions as they occur to them, not when it is most convenient for a parent to answer them. As a result, every parent has suffered through the experience of having a small child ask in a crowded bus, elevator, or movie-house lobby, (always in a loud voice, it seems), "Why does that lady's stomach stick out that way?" or "Why does that man only have one arm?" The point to remember is that you are the only one in the crowd likely to be really distressed. The child isn't, the pregnant woman isn't, and the man with only one arm has probably heard the question dozens of times before. Try to answer as matter-of-factly as possible, or, if the question is truly too embarrassing to deal with at that moment, say it is not a good thing to talk about on the bus or in the elevator but that you will be glad to discuss it when you get home. Don't forget to do it!

Children's questions are not bad. It is important to make them understand that it's the timing, not the question, that is unwelcome. It's even more important to let them know that most of the time you're glad to answer any and all questions they care to ask. Parents who get that feeling across early will be the people children turn to for information and support.

On the other hand, answering children's questions about sexuality untruthfully or not at all will not, as parents may once have thought, protect their children from the realities of life and dissuade them from unacceptable behavior. Instead it teaches them that they cannot depend on parents to be supportive in this area and that they must look for information and guidance somewhere else.

LISTENING, HEARING—AND MORE LISTENING

One of the authors of this book will always remember a long-ago encounter because of the lesson it taught her about parenting in general and listening in particular. Visiting a strange city, she was invited to lunch by a fellow writer she had never met. They had many friends and interests in common and were deep in an enjoyable conversation when the hostess's young daughter arrived home from school. The visitor, not yet a parent herself, was a bit surprised when the mother asked the little girl to join them and for at least ten minutes gave her all her attention. The questions she asked and the comments she offered made it clear to the child (and the visitor) that whatever happened to the daughter was of paramount importance to her mother and definitely took precedence over entertaining a stranger.

It is not always easy to muster that much interest about tales of the third grade. But if young children have the feeling that parents are genuinely interested in what is happening in their world, they are more likely to be open about it in later years, the years when parents really want to know what their children are thinking and doing.

Children know that when parents don't listen, it is not a sign they don't love them. Children are remarkably understanding. But they definitely know parents love them when they *do* listen, so that may be what is most important.

Besides showing real interest, another component of good listening is being sensitive to the unspoken message that is sometimes behind the spoken words. People often say only indirectly the things that are really on their minds. At the parents' meeting we mentioned earlier, for instance, a nurse brought up a conversation she and her thirteen-year-old daughter had a day earlier. "My daughter came home with the latest issue of *Seventeen* magazine and slapped it down on the kitchen table," she said. "Two of the cover lines were 'I Had an Abortion' and 'I Kept My Baby.' The articles were by two unmarried teenagers. Janny, my daughter, said, 'You ought to be proud of me, Mom. I read both those articles . . .' "

It wasn't hard for the group to agree on what Janny was trying to tell her mother, though her method was a bit roundabout. They decided she was in effect saying: "I am thinking about sex these days and all the things it involves, and I am trying to get more information. You should be proud of me for being so sensible."

Janny's mother also sensed behind the offhand remark Janny's unspoken curiosity about her mother's feelings with regard to teen pregnancy, and she gladly accepted the silent invitation to talk about it. If she hadn't been listening carefully, she could have missed a useful opportunity.

Listening becomes a more complex affair when children get older. It means different things to them at different times. They want parents to respond to their news of the day with more than a grunt. "If I say anything to my dad, all he does is say 'Great!' or 'I don't know,' " a somewhat typical fifteen-year-old girl complains. If parents find what they have to say is that boring, these youngsters figure, then why bother?

Another, even more important kind of listening parents can provide is in situations where their children have problems and need help. In this case, besides interest they want support, maybe sympathy, maybe advice, and definitely not "a hassle." Parents who are good at that kind of listening are truly special to their children.

Finally, adolescents want parents to listen during the inevitable confrontations, head buttings, or power struggles about whether Joe can have the car tonight, when Corinne may or may not date, why Andy failed math, and on and on.

Judging by a sample of high schoolers we questioned, more teens than not consider their parents good listeners, at least some of the time. Fewer than one in five said that neither parent was a good listener. However, their answers made it clear they interpret "listening" in at least all the ways we have outlined. From their comments, the portrait of a good parent-listener is someone who:

1. Doesn't yell at me.
2. Doesn't interrupt the minute I get started.
3. Is interested in what I'm saying.
4. Is willing to see it from my side.
5. Will try to help me solve my problems or will answer my questions.
6. Doesn't bear down on me to say more than I want to.

PRIVACY: EVERYONE NEEDS IT

Parents impress on their offspring at an early age the fact that adults require privacy of various sorts: "Please don't come into our bedroom without knocking." "Daddy likes to be alone when he's in the bathroom." "Run along, honey; I want to talk to your grandmother privately." Or "Play in your room—I need a little time to myself." All of these are requests that parents routinely make. And it's right that they do this. If children are to live comfortably with others, they must learn to respect other people's needs for privacy.

Children also have a right to expect the same from their parents: "Please don't come into *my* room without knocking—or search it while I'm at school, or read my mail, or listen in on my telephone conversations" are reasonable requests. But about a quarter of all the teenagers we have talked to say these types of parental habits are among the biggest causes of discord between them and one or both of their parents. Young teenagers tend to be sensitive, self-conscious, and alienated from almost all adults at times. So privacy may become more of an issue.

Privacy, after all, is *not* an exclusively adult privilege. Children need it as much as grown-ups, though they sometimes have a harder time achieving it. They need it for a number of reasons. The first is that a desire for privacy represents a young child's attempt to develop independence and confirm that he is his "own person." A child needs to know that adults respect his/her independence. "How *could* you tell Aunt Jane I have to get braces?" a little girl angrily accuses her mother. "It's none of her business!"

What seems neither a very important nor a particularly intimate revelation to an adult can appear quite the opposite to the child involved. It is *her* right, not her mother's, to decide who should know of this private matter. She feels her mother has betrayed a confidence. And that is too bad, because when a youngster learns that a parent cannot be trusted with confidences, he or she is likely to become even more uncommunicative.

Another kind of privacy young children need is a recognition of their growing modesty. This modesty indicates a developing awareness of the child's own sexuality and society's attitudes toward it. When a little boy protests his mother's continuing to undress him or a little girl complains about her mother's barging into the bathroom while she is in the tub, they are reflecting lessons they have been taught, and their feelings deserve consideration.

As they mature, the privacy children want for themselves extends, as they are quick to let parents know, to their rooms, their mail, their telephone calls, and—most importantly—to what they are thinking and doing. This is partly because of their growing need to become independent from their parents and partly because they suspect that at least some of the things they are thinking and doing are likely to provoke parental disapproval or, as they put it, cause "a hassle." Every reader can undoubtedly supply a few examples from youthful memory. At moments of exasperation with a teenager, a parent might do well to recall such times.

In the meantime parents are worrying, often with good reason, that their teenagers are thinking and doing things that might get them into trouble or make them very unhappy. Parents feel that if they only knew the facts, they could offer advice or help or prohibitions that would be useful. Perhaps they *could* offer such help, if they are able to take a rebuff without becoming hostile and if they are willing to try to discuss matters again at a more opportune moment. Above all, we think, parents should be sure they don't make their teenagers feel guilty about needing privacy.

We asked a sample of seventy boys and girls, ages fifteen and sixteen, whether they feel their parents invade their privacy, and we received a heartening "no" from half of them. But we also read a share of comments (mostly from girls) like these:

"If I don't tell my mom everything I do when I go out with my friends or my boyfriends, or if I have a problem and don't talk to her about it but would rather go in my room and talk on the phone, she gets mad at me."

"Questions, questions, and more questions is all I hear from my parents," a fifteen-year-old boy wrote in obvious exasperation.

"I feel they invade my privacy when they make me tell them things I don't want to" is a comment from a sixteen-year-old girl.

Kids this age will fight hard to protect their psychological territory. Understandably they are most insistent upon their privacy where sexual matters are concerned. Teenage girls, particularly, often feel it is too risky to discuss with parents, much as they may want information or advice.

"Anything I tell my mother she tells my father right away, and he gets furious" is a comment sex educators frequently hear from teenagers.

On the other hand, of the sixty-seven teenagers who answered our question "Do you believe it would be better for parents to know if a teenager is having sex?" just over half the girls and just under half the boys answered either "yes" or "maybe." The reasons they gave most often were that if parents knew, they could advise the girls about contraception, be supportive if there were emotional problems, and help out (as most adolescents recognize they would have to) if a girl became pregnant. Like many an adult, they obviously would like to have it both ways. As syndicated columnist Ellen Goodman has written, *"Teens push alternately for independence and protection. . . . They are hostile to interference and frightened by indifference."*

The parents who enjoy their teenagers' confidence are those who respect their privacy by not expecting to be told *everything,* by not pushing for more information than is volunteered, and by not prying into a child's activities (room searching, mail reading, eavesdropping, etc.). Many kids complain: "Any time I ask my mom or dad anything at all about sex, they think it means I'm doing it." The parents may or may not be correct. If they respond personally to impersonal questions or genuine requests for information, they're going to discourage any further dialogue. *Impersonal* conversations about sexual matters, on the other hand, can be enormously helpful to teenagers. There is so much they want to know, so much about which they need reassurance—even to feel it is okay to ask about sexual matters in the first place.

Many of the teenagers in our sample who replied emphatically that their parents never invaded their privacy added that it was "because they trust me." Teenagers may rarely volunteer the information to Mom and Dad, but most of them care deeply about parental trust. When parents trust their children, they should let them know it; if they feel they can't, they should look into the reasons and try to find a remedy. They need to be sure, in turn, that their children can trust them to respect their privacy, too.

When parents respect their children's needs, it sends a message to the teenagers that their parents trust their ability and judgment to make sound decisions—not necessarily limited to decisions on sexual matters.

Parents can and do learn to "trust and let go."

CHAPTER 4

Growing Up with Self-Esteem

The way people feel about themselves colors the way they feel about others and the world they live in. These feelings start developing in infancy. Babies begin to feel self-esteem when someone finds them worth feeding and cuddling and making comfortable. It continues to grow as toddlers learn new skills and receive praise as a result. When a two-year-old girl hears her mother say, "My, you did that really well," she feels terrific about herself. This is the way she begins to believe in her own competence. Children who grow up with a conviction that they are loved and that they are competent are well equipped as adolescents and as adults to deal with people and situations on their own terms.

A great deal of attention has been paid in recent years to the connection between adolescent self-esteem and adolescent sexual behavior, and the facts and figures certainly seem to support the existence of the connection. Feeling good about themselves allows boys and girls to feel they are in charge of their own lives, that they *belong*—in a family, in a group, in a community—and that they can be like the people they admire and can achieve the goals they aspire to.

Boys and girls who think poorly of themselves don't feel they are in charge of their lives. They are willing to accept the minimum, settle for any relationship, no matter how damaging, because anything is better than nothing. Adolescents with low self-esteem don't expect to be liked or respected. They expect to be used, and they often are.

It is unrealistic to assume that teenagers who think they are "nothing" will be able to see any future worth working toward. "What difference does it make if I get pregnant?" a fifteen-year-old is apt to reason. "I didn't want to finish school anyway."

They may be tempted to use sex to gain friends or status. Boys may think that by exploiting girls and becoming known as "studs" they will impress their peers, while girls often hope that having a sexual relationship will give them new importance in the eyes of others.

Because the development of self-esteem is a continuing process, the way even the most devoted parents handle their children's upbringing can do a lot to either foster or stifle that development.

Toddlers need to practice new skills and become increasingly independent, no matter how tempting it is to save time by doing things for them or to remain powerful by keeping them dependent. As they grow, children need to be encouraged to develop talents and special abilities. It is a great comfort to the teenager tortured by self-doubt to know that he or she does something better than most people.

Making their own decisions is another way youngsters develop a sense of competence. It pays to encourage them whenever it's appropriate. Obviously an eight-year-old can't be allowed to decide whether she will go to school or not on a given morning, but she can decide which outfit she will wear. Becoming comfortable with making decisions helps children take the next step—to accepting responsibility.

Everyone likes to be praised for their actions. Children have a particular need for such praise. Their parents' approval is the only measure they have of their own value. On the other hand, when they mess up or do something that is wrong, it's important to let them know that it is the deed and not the child the parent is disapproving of. Children have a hard time understanding that they are separate from their behavior, so to them disliked behavior is the same as a dislike of themselves.

The mother we described in the section on "listening," who showed so much interest in her daughter's day at school was also contributing to her child's self-esteem by not treating her like a "second-class citizen," something parents are often guilty of doing without being conscious of it. Her mother's response let the little girl know she was as important as an adult.

As children reach adolescence, craving for acceptance—by their peers, by themselves, by their parents—becomes almost vital to survival. At a time when they need most to be just like everybody else—because they believe that if they're not they must be "weird," a "freak," or "gross"—they are dismayed to find themselves *least* like anyone else. Each one is growing and developing at his or her own rate, and the results are more unnerving to them than adults can possibly remember. How often, after all, does the average adult agonize over whether his body is "normal"? Teenagers probably do it half a dozen times a day, or every time they're reminded of their height, breasts, penis size, or skin condition.

They have a tremendous need for reassurance that the time span of pubertal changes varies widely and that their growth and development is normal for them. Pubertal changes start at different times for different people and, once begun, occur at different rates. Teenagers need to be praised—honestly—for their strong points, both physical and behavioral, and given help—uncritically—in compensating for or strengthening their weak ones.

Recently we asked a group of teenagers what their parents did that made them feel best about themselves. They worded their answers in different ways, but the phrases we encountered most often were: "they encourage my efforts," "trust me to make the right decisions," "support my ideas and projects," "don't tear me down," and (from a fifteen-year-old male) the impressive statement that "both parents are supportive of me by allowing me to control most of my quotidian activities, and the responsibility is a great esteem builder." (We must admit it was *not* an esteem builder for us to have to consult the dictionary to learn that "quotidian" means "occurring daily.")

A young friend of ours put it this way: "Mom gives me the feeling she respects my judgment. For instance, she is always so accepting of my friends that they feel good about coming to my house, and that makes me feel good about myself. I must be okay if I have okay friends."

And it is terribly important for people her age to know they are okay. As Dorothy Briggs, a psychologist and family counselor has written: *"The evidence suggests that the best insulation against indiscriminate sexual behavior when the herd instinct runs high in adolescence—when sexual urges are intense—is a high degree of personal worth."*

CHAPTER 5

Letting Children Know It Is Safe to Be Sexual

One reason parents often falter when it comes to talking to their children about sexuality is that they are anxious and uncertain about *what* they should discuss *when.*

It may be helpful to remember that children think about things, perceive situations, and respond to information differently than adults do. A three-year-old, for instance, is unable to conceptualize how babies are created; a four-year-old who happens to see parents having intercourse may think they are fighting; a five-year-old who is told that "Daddy planted a seed in Mommy" is apt to form a frightening picture of some agricultural event taking place inside her.

The psychosexual development of children was first charted and divided into distinct stages in the early part of this century. In the 1960s, the behaviorist Jean Piaget, who devoted his career to studying how children think, developed a theory of "stages" of thinking ability. A number of researchers have built on this framework; their studies confirm that children are indeed born sexual and that their thinking about sexual matters and their sexual feelings (two quite separate things) change in predictable ways as they grow. The following brief sketches of these developmental stages may be useful in helping parents understand how their children think and feel and why they are acting as they are.

An infant begins to learn about love from Day One—from the way her mother and father touch her and hold her, from the tone of their voice when they speak to her, from how comfortable they make her. This, says Freud, is the beginning of sexuality. Feeding, especially, but the total atmosphere that surrounds caring for an infant spells either love and pleasure or lack of them to the infant. Normal curiosity makes babies start to explore their own bodies when they are young. Some of them also learn early that it feels better to touch some parts than others. Even quite young infants have been observed achieving what appears to be an orgasm.

By eighteen months babies have developed an understanding of cause and effect, according to Piaget. If every time a toddler touches his genitals his hand is slapped, he will probably stop doing that—at least when anyone is around. (He may touch his genitals in private—and feel guilty.) When the child is a little older, parental disapproval of this activity will convey the message that what is actually normal and natural behavior is in some way wicked. That is too bad because it may plant the idea that obtaining pleasure from genital behavior is unacceptable.

As boys and girls begin to understand that they belong to one sex or another, between the ages of two and three, they face a vitally important learning task. The impression they form now of what being male or female means is going to affect their future behavior, their relationships, and ultimately their sexual responses.

One way children test these impressions is to imitate adult behavior. Little boys often try to imitate Daddy shaving; probably every woman alive tried at some point to urinate standing up.

The connections between learning to use the toilet and sexual perceptions have been known for many years. As a child's body is all-important to him, so are the products that come out of it. If he gains the impression from his parents' attitudes during toilet training that these products are dirty or disgusting, he may believe the places they came out of are too.

Probably the sight most likely to upset parents during the preschool years is to come upon children undressing each other, examining each other's genitals, or even "playing doctor." By adult standards this kind of behavior appears to have adult sexual connotations. It certainly doesn't look sweet and innocent like "playing tea party."

What we forget is that such behavior doesn't have the same meaning for the children involved as it does for the onlooking adult. Preschool children are extremely curious about bodies, their own and those of others, and this checking out of differences is a natural part of their developing sexual identification. (We've never heard it suggested, but it occurs to us that "playing doctor" might also be a small child's way of relieving feelings of resentment about having adults examine him or her.)

Our advice to parents is not to overreact and thereby instill feelings of guilt and shame about an activity that is essentially harmless and in all likelihood will be abandoned when the children's curiosity is satisfied. Children who are obsessively interested may be reacting to a pattern of silence within the family about sexual matters. This behavior might well be forestalled by taking the opportunity at bath time to casually point out and name genitalia and explain that they are different in boys and girls.

A three-year-old is not too young to have the anatomical differences between the sexes explained. By that age he or she is probably already wondering and worrying about them. Little girls need to be reassured that it is right for them not to have a penis and that the sexual organs they do have are equally desirable and worthy. Little boys too should understand that there is a purpose in the sexes being made differently. This information is so basic and nonerotic that it shouldn't be any harder to talk about than differences in hair or eye or skin color.

Modern studies of young children have made it increasingly clear how important it is to use the correct terms for body parts from the beginning. Using vague or made-up words for the genitals conveys the impression that there is something "wrong" with them, that they are unmentionable, evil, or, as one study of preschool children showed, not real parts of the body like the nose or the elbow because they have no real names.

Not knowing the correct words can also make it pretty hard to communicate when it is important to do so. Another study, of seven hundred English-speaking children, turned up sixty-five different terms for "penis"! If a child is trying to describe an injury or abuse, inexact descriptions like "down there" or "my bottom" are definitely not useful.

From three years old on, most children become deeply interested in the question of where babies come from. Since they have no notion of adult sexuality, there is no need to go into the physical and emotional aspects of intercourse. Answers should start as simply as "It grows in a special place inside the mother" the first time around and progress slowly over the years as a child's ability to grasp the concept develops.

Dr. Anne C. Bernstein, a clinical psychologist, has done extensive studies of the six levels of thinking that children progress through with respect to the origin of babies.

In one study she asked over one hundred American children from fairly sophisticated and educated families, "How do people get babies?" Most of these children's parents thought they had explained it adequately and were amazed by the answers their offspring gave.

At about three or four years old (Level 1), a child cannot perceive any cause for a baby. It simply has always existed—maybe somewhere else, the child imagines.

At Level 2, roughly between four and eight (there can be considerable variation in chronological age), children begin to attribute babies to some cause but most often believe they are assembled by adults or manufactured like store-bought goods.

Dr. Bernstein has said her interviews with young children make it hard for her to believe they could have been told the answers they give. Instead their replies seem "to be put together out of answers gathered and given, held together with childish logic that reflects their understanding of the world."

At Level 3, around eight years of age, children can recognize that the father is involved in the baby's creation and have some notion of the mechanics of intercourse, but they don't put the whole process together in a coherent fashion.

Level 4 (around eight to ten) is the first one at which children show embarrassment about being asked where babies come from, Dr. Bernstein notes. They can describe purely physical causes of conception, but they still don't understand why genetic material must unite to start the life process. This may also be true of Level 5 children, ages eleven and twelve. At both these levels children need to have it explained that the embryo does not begin to exist until the sperm and egg meet and fuse.

At Level 6, by the time of puberty, boys and girls can usually describe a reasonably accurate picture of how people get babies—provided they have been given it.

Another study of children's understanding is illuminating in another way. In 1974 sex educator Patricia Barthalow-Koch set out to learn whether the compulsory sex education offered in schools in Sweden "enhances the fundamental knowledge and accompanying attitudes about sexuality for children ages seven to eight more than the typical American approach."

She asked a group of American second-graders and a comparable class of Swedish second-graders to draw pictures of where babies come from and how they are born, and then to explain their pictures privately to a teacher.

The explanations of the American children ranged from God's will (with no human involvement), to eating a certain type of food, and even to dreaming. Not one of them mentioned any type of male involvement except for the child who said, "The doctor cuts her open. It hurts a lot."

In the Swedish class, on the other hand, eleven out of fifteen children drew pictures of reproduction as taking place through sexual intercourse. They also grasped the concepts of contraception, childbirth, and parenting. In all their pictures, mothers, fathers, and babies are smiling!

What this research points out is that it is terribly important to answer young children's questions about reproduction as simply, honestly, and clearly as possible. Dr. Bernstein has suggested that a useful way to start is by asking them what *their* ideas of a baby's origin are in order to get a feeling for their level of comprehension. She and other educators also make the point that because young children are so literal-minded, the analogies often used to explain birth can be misleading, confusing, or even frightening to them. Eggs are seen as the hard-shelled food people eat; seed is seen as the beginning of a plant growing in soil in mother's stomach, and so on. (We offer several ways to phrase these answers in the chapters ahead.)

A well-known characteristic of children at the first and second levels of sexual understanding, around three or four, is that they are likely to be intensely attached to the parent of the opposite sex and even have jealous feelings about the same-sex parent. Although they are not capable of adult thinking, they are undoubtedly sexual beings, capable of tenderness, devotion, and jealousy—all feelings associated with adult sexuality.

This is also the age, since they are now physically mobile but not yet physically modest (adult principles of "morality" still being undeveloped) when they want to snuggle in bed with parents, join them in the bathroom, watch them getting dressed, or handle their genitals. How all these situations are dealt with must depend on individual family feelings. The degree of comfort or discomfort parents exhibit probably gives children a stronger sexual message than their actual words. Parents can comfortably and appropriately set privacy limits.

Between five and seven, children's attitudes about parents are likely to change. They give up wanting to "marry" mother or father and want more closeness with the same-sex parent. They are also quite sure by now of their own masculinity or femininity and may enter into a period of claiming to despise children of the opposite sex. Masturbation is quite common at this age. If children are openly handling their genitals, it is an appropriate time to talk about it. Reassure them that it is not wrong, but explain that it is one of the things people do in private.

Eight- to twelve-year-olds are busy with social development. They are separating from parents but becoming increasingly preoccupied with what people their own age think of them. Pubertal changes can also begin at any time during these years, and parents should thoroughly explain these changes to both boys and girls well in advance, and in particular should reassure the child that they are normal and desirable. We will talk about this more specifically in Part II.

Anna Freud wisely pointed out many years ago that no child can help but be occupied with sexual concerns in the years before puberty. That is more true today. The best thing we can do for our children is to make them feel safe about showing these concerns and feelings and encourage them to continue asking questions throughout their growing years.

If parents don't work to develop an environment for their children to talk freely about sex and sexuality, their youngsters are likely to learn about this vital part of their lives in less than desirable ways. Asked to describe anonymously the primary source of their sexual knowledge, these college freshmen and sophomores wrote:

> I learned how the genital organs function in a seventh-grade health class, but I never knew how the two interacted.

> . . . Through pictures in dirty magazines and pictures the boys would draw. My parents would have been too embarrassed to talk to me. I'm not saying this was right of them; I

believe it was very wrong. If parents feel this way, they should have the child attend some kind of sex education class.

My mother never told me anything, but my father was always worried I'd get pregnant. When I was thirteen, they wanted to know what I knew about birth control, but they never told me why it was necessary.

Sex education was taboo in our school. We all learned the same way—by doing.

Strictly gutter/street. My parents never talked to me.

My knowledge about sexual matters was practically nil till I came to college and found out boys want more than kisses. Most of my knowledge has come from my boyfriend, but I still don't know everything.

I learned about menstruation from my best friend when I was eight. I was flabbergasted my own mother had it happen to her every month and never told me!!

Mostly from my boyfriend. We were both inexperienced virgins when we first slept together three years ago.

Out of forty students, seven said their mothers had been their primary source of information; two said they had been the secondary source, and three said both parents had told them what they wanted to know. Of all the comments, one we at Planned Parenthood wish we had heard more often was: *Whenever I wanted to know anything, I went straight to my mother. Ever since I was a small child, she has honestly tried to make me understand whatever I wondered about.*

PART II

The Facts

CHAPTER 6

What They Want to Know— Preschoolers to High Schoolers

As discussed earlier, children are curious about different aspects of sexuality at different ages. Young children are interested primarily in such practical questions as "Where did I come from?" or "How does the baby get out of the mother?" It is usually quite a bit later before they question, "How did it get in?"

Preadolescent and adolescent children, on the other hand, need not only solid information about the physical aspects but want to know about the more intangible facets of human sexuality as well as the moral, emotional, and social values involved.

It is also true that children's interest may focus fleetingly on some topic and, if their curiosity is satisfied at that point, may disappear only to emerge again when they are able to understand more about the matter and have a wider context in which to place it.

Menstruation is such an example. A mother may be upset when a four- or five-year-old finds tampons or sanitary napkins in the bathroom and asks what they are for. She feels the sub-

ject is inappropriate and too complex to discuss with a young
child. In fact it is an opportunity for a mother to lay the groundwork, simply and reassuringly, for the in-depth discussion she
will need to have with her daughter or son a few years later.
About all she needs to tell a small child is something like:

> "When you were growing inside me, you needed a special
> place. My body prepared that place. Every month, for me and
> for every woman, our bodies get ready. When no egg and
> sperm come together, my body cleans out that special place
> and starts again. The lining, which is like blood, slips out
> through the same opening that you did. Since it's sort of
> messy, I use the pad to keep from getting my clothes spotted
> on those few days."

If a mother gets across the feeling that this is a normal,
healthy, good thing that happens to grown-up women, the child
is likely to find her explanation satisfying.

A situation as common as this one shows yet again that sexuality education really has to be a continuing process. It is
unrealistic to believe that one recitation of facts can suffice for
all time or that what a five-year-old needs to know will be
useful to a child twice that age. Many parents, though, seem to
believe one telling is enough, as this wistful comment from one
of the college students we quoted earlier makes clear: "When I
was about eight, my mother told me where babies came from. I
guess it was pretty admirable of her to come right out with it,
but we haven't actually talked about it since then."

In this section we will try to give parents a time frame for
talking to their children—an indication of the kinds of information about sexuality that children are interested in at different
stages of their development and some practical help in providing that information comfortably. All the questions or situations we include for different age groups have been asked
about or described by children of those ages—in nursery
school, in sex education classes, in Planned Parenthood centers. Undoubtedly we could collect hundreds more—the human

imagination is almost limitless—but those we have chosen to include seem most representative of what children are thinking about at different ages and of the types of answers which help them learn about sexuality.

THE PRESCHOOLER

To know what aspects of sexuality interest little children, one has only to watch the games they play with one another.

- They need to be sure of their own gender: "You be the mommy, and I'll be the daddy."
- They are interested in learning how the parts of the body that are normally covered by clothes look: hence the universal game of "doctor."
- They act out situations to test their ideas of how things happen: "Pretend the baby is trying to get out of your stomach and I will be the doctor and cut a hole for it."
- They explore their own bodies to learn their capabilities and what feels good.

These are the clues a sensitive parent can use to satisfy a small child's natural need to know about life: Provide your youngster with relaxed opportunities to see what other children and opposite-sex children look like naked—at bath time or getting ready for bed—and point out the anatomical differences. Explain to little ones at these times what their sexual body parts are for. Supply the right names for all body parts and mention that the way they look will change as children grow. If you make a habit of using correct names, they will come to seem more natural than "weewee" or "tutu." If one of your friends is pregnant, ask her to let your child "feel the baby move." Show your children a newborn baby if that is possible. Explain simply how it was born.

Children will probably not be curious about how a baby gets inside the mother until they are five or six, and explanations of intercourse at that age can be brief. We think that all discussions should include the idea that intercourse is loving and caring, not simply baby making. This concept remains hard for children to grasp for quite a few more years, and their interest in the explanation may be less than overwhelming. As one eight-year-old told a child psychologist, "I never really got around to how people have babies because I have loads of other things to do."

Small children's questions come at such unexpected times and can be so imaginative that many parents say they find it helpful to formulate answers to some of the most predictable ones ahead of time. If prepared, they are less flustered than they would be if caught off guard. Following are two examples of questions small children often ask and ways in which they might be answered:

Why can't I pee standing up like Daddy?
"You're a girl and you'll grow into a woman, like me. Daddy is a man—a grown-up boy. Boys and men have penises and their pee—the real word is "urine"—comes out of their penises. We have vaginas and another little opening called the urethra. Our urine comes out of that little opening. It's between our legs, so we sit down to urinate."

Why does that lady's stomach stick out so far?
"She is going to have a baby very soon. All women have a special place in their bodies called a uterus. Before you were born, you were growing in my uterus, and my stomach looked just as big as that lady's does."

Other questions that almost every child between the ages of three and six can be guaranteed to ask are:

- *What's that?* (Pointing to the father's penis.) "My penis."
- *Why don't I have one?* "Because you're a girl, and girls have vulvas and vaginas. Men and boys don't."
- *What are those?* (Boy or girl pointing to mother's breasts.) "My breasts."

- *Will I have them too?* "Yes." (Or "No," depending on the sex of the child.)
- *How are babies made?* "When the mother and father want to have a child he puts his penis in her vagina, and they make love in a special way."
- *How long does a baby stay in the mother's stomach?* "A baby grows in a special place inside the mother, called the uterus—not in her stomach. In nine months it is born."
- *How does it get out?* "Through a special opening, called the vagina."
- *What does it feel like to be born? Does it hurt?* "Not the baby. The mother's muscles work very hard, and it is sometimes painful for her for a short time."
- *Can I watch you and Daddy* (or *Mommy) making a baby?*

Probably the only question on this list that might give a parent pause is the last one. To the child it doesn't imply anything more than asking why her mother has breasts. It should be enough to say simply, "No, I'm afraid you can't. When Daddy and I make a baby, it is a time we want to be alone—all parents do—and not have anyone watching. But right now is there anything more you would like to know about how they are made?"

Children need knowledge in order to survive. Their curiosity about sexual matters is just a small part of their curiosity about all that happens in their world. When the curiosity isn't satisfied, it is like an itch that isn't scratched. When it is, the information can be uneventfully stored away for future need.

THE EARLY GRADE SCHOOL YEARS (AGES SIX TO NINE)

From around six years or so, many children become newly reticent about asking adults questions having to do with anything sexual. Sigmund Freud believed this reticence meant children were entering into a phase he called "latency." He theorized that during these years, a child actually repressed sexual feelings and fantasies as being dangerous, only to have them reemerge in adult form at adolescence—the "genital" stage.

A simpler explanation, more widely accepted today, is that as children move into the world outside the family, they become aware of what adults find acceptable in the way of child behavior and conversation and become wary of expressing ideas or asking questions that might cause trouble. Every parent is familiar with the hectic giggling that can go on when a group of six- to eight-year-olds are together and how abruptly it can stop when an adult is sighted. It's a pretty safe bet that the trigger for the giggling has something to do with sex.

Contrary to Freud's latency theory, the average grade-schooler is aware of and is probably quite curious about a wide variety of sexual topics, certainly more than he or she was when younger. The limited world of the preschool years and the young child's preoccupation with self is rapidly augmented in the grade school years by a range of outside influences and sexual references. The intensity or pressure of these wider sexual influences was unheard of twenty-five years ago when today's parents were growing up.

At the same time youngsters are increasingly being exposed to sexual references, they are also becoming more "socialized," and thus conscious, probably for the first time, that certain kinds of questions make parents uncomfortable. So the questions are not asked of them.

It's tempting for parents who are uneasy discussing sexual matters to take a child's silence at face value and to conclude with relief that there is nothing he or she really wants to know just now. Parents who do that are deluding themselves. Any child who is not totally protected from the adult world is aware that things exist called rape, AIDS, child abuse, homosexuality, abortion, and pornography, to name just a few bewildering aspects of sexuality that crop up on the evening news.

Not long ago *The Wall Street Journal* reported on a survey taken of a group of six- and seven-year-olds to learn which TV commercials were reaching their targeted audiences. In the process it was also learned that while these young viewers may not know who Dan Rather is, they are well acquainted with J. R. Ewing, Michael Jackson, and Cyndi Lauper, that they believe "drinking alcohol is bad because it makes you drive and then you crash," and that "generic" is something you spread on bread. This is just one of dozens of possibilities that show how much children take in every day without really understanding.

In families where sexuality has always been a comfortable subject as children grow up, they may continue to ask questions that show their perfectly natural interest in what is happening in the world around them. This certainly makes sex education easier for their parents. But even when children don't question, parents need to keep talking. Parents often find it easier to discuss sexual topics that have no personal relevance for the child, even though he or she needs to understand them. A newspaper headline "Woman Raped at Knife Point" is an opening for asking if the youngster knows what "rape" means and, if not, to explain. The same is true of all the sex-linked subjects we just cited. Sometimes the need for explanation can be more immediate. One young mother we know felt that her seven-year-old daughter deserved an honest, if simplified, explanation of AIDS when a close family friend died of the disease.

When sexual discussions become more complex and specific, the discomfort level frequently rises on both sides. A more verbal six-year-old or a quieter eight-year-old may ask, "When do boys begin to make sperm?" "What are periods?" "Do men ever marry each other?" "When can a girl have a baby?" These are typical of the many questions that occur to every grade-schooler. Certainly these are legitimate questions, and whether they are voiced or not, correct answers need to be supplied. One way to break the ice is to ask children how much they know about subjects you surmise are of concern to them.

Even their shortest reply provides you with an opening to give them more information.

And don't think it won't be absorbed! Parents often feel frustrated when the sexual information they have imparted with so much difficulty is greeted with such typical reactions of grade-schoolers as stony silence and averted eyes, "Oh, Ma, I know about that stuff," or a simple "Yuck!" It's natural to want a more positive response, but lack of it by no means indicates that the information didn't register with your child. It may be some time before a parent's monologue turns into a parent-child dialogue, but it is a goal definitely worth striving for. A one-sided conversation, awkward as it feels, may be the only way of eventually achieving it. It never hurts, either, to let a child know you find the situation awkward and would appreciate a little feedback. "When I was little, my parents never talked to me about these things, so you and I are learning together" is an admission that can't help but evoke understanding.

Conversations between adults to which children are allowed to listen without having to participate can be instructive and nonthreatening. Many adults automatically fall silent if a youngster enters the room when anything sexual is being discussed. Dropping the subject may be wasting a useful opportunity for imparting information. Silence also promotes the confusing idea to a child that anything sexual is secret. Children need to have a framework in which to evaluate the information they are acquiring. Unfortunately the framework for sexual matters that society seems to expose is a glorification of exploitative or sensational sex rather than support of loving, responsible sexuality.

Whether they actually ask their questions, grade school children are almost universally curious about such topics as "How does a baby come out?"

An appropriate answer might be: "There is a special opening between a woman's legs that is called the vagina. After a baby has been in its mother's uterus for nine months, it's ready to be born and the vagina stretches to let it slip out."

The other part of the question, which may come before or after, is of course, "How does the baby get in?"

An answer to this one depends on what parents have already told children, when they were younger. The simplest answer is to say that when a husband and wife are loving each other in a special way, the man puts his penis in the woman's vagina and some fluid is released through the penis. There are many sperm cells in the fluid. If one of them meets an egg cell inside the mother, new life can begin to grow.

"How come some babies are girls and some are boys?" is another common concern of grade schoolers.

"It depends on which sperm cell from the father enters the mother's egg cell" might be your answer.

Children in this age group first begin to be preoccupied with being "normal" and consequently are interested in all non-normal things such as twins, Siamese twins, or deformities. If a child asks how Siamese twins came about, a parent might first explain that there are two kinds of twins—those resulting from the union of one sperm and one egg and those from the union of two sperms and two eggs. In the case of Siamese twins, when the fertilized egg divides to make two identical beings, it does not divide completely and the fetuses remain attached as they grow. It is also a good idea to mention that this is extremely rare. The way you answer a question, as well as what you answer, conveys a message to the child. The old adage "Actions speak louder than words" certainly applies to parent-child communication about sex and sexuality.

"What is puberty?" children often want to know.

They could be told that puberty marks the beginning of a stage of growth called adolescence when the glands of the body begin to manufacture hormones—substances that cause them to develop into women or men. Every boy and girl goes through it. Different bodies grow at different rates, so one person may enter puberty at age nine while another may not start till age fifteen.

THE PRETEEN YEARS (AGES NINE TO TWELVE)

Here is how one young woman recalls learning about menstruation: "When I asked my mother what a period was, she gave me three books and sent me to my room to read them. I was so embarrassed. The whole thing seemed so gross. I never asked her anything more about it."

Unfortunately, that young woman is not unique. A great many girls and boys go through puberty with the attitude that the changes taking place in their bodies are "gross" or shameful. Very likely they wouldn't feel that way if they had been given the information they needed when they needed it—that is, well before the changes of puberty begin. Parents can start talking about growth and development to their children when they start school. That conversation about "growing up" lays the groundwork for later discussions about changing bodies.

Nine years old is not too young to begin talking with children specifically about menstruation and nocturnal emissions. Most girls have their first period between the ages of eleven and fourteen, but they can begin earlier. Boys' nocturnal emissions usually begin when they are about thirteen or fourteen, but again, wide variation in age is possible. A child who has been given no preparation for the experience can find it deeply upsetting. It is hard to imagine a ten-year-old who hasn't heard something from peers about these two subjects, but "something from peers" falls far short of what a youngster approaching puberty needs to know.

At no other time in their lives do human beings undergo such profound and potentially unnerving bodily changes as they do at puberty. At no other time are children as much in need of understanding and sensitive reassurance that what is happening to them is okay. Almost every aspect of puberty can be cause for alarm. Some girls, for instance, are so appalled at the sight of the first little pubic hairs sprouting that they pluck them out with tweezers!

One of the most difficult aspects for youngsters to handle is the wide variation in the rate of physical development at a given age. The question "Am I normal?" becomes almost an obsession now—and no wonder. Imagine being the only girl in the class who hasn't started menstruating or the only boy in the locker room who has no pubic hair. The variations on this theme are almost endless.

"Puberty was godawful," a young man commented. "I wish my parents had filled me in a little about what was going on with me. Once in a while one of them would say something like 'Don't worry, son' about my acne. Big help! That was among the least of my problems."

Along with all the stresses caused by having to learn to deal with a "new" body shape and size come those caused by needing to learn how to deal with family and friends, who are responding to this new "growing-up person"—and with one's self! Adolescence isn't called stormy for nothing.

Despite the wide variations in rates of physical development, there is a definite maturational sequence that parents should be aware of.

For girls the order is:

- Breasts start to enlarge.
- Straight pubic hair appears.
- A growth spurt occurs.
- Pubic hair becomes kinky.
- Menstruation begins.
- Hair appears under the arms.

The corresponding changes in boys are:

- Testes and penis begin to grow.
- Straight pubic hair appears.
- Early voice changes take place.
- Ejaculation becomes possible.

- Pubic hair becomes kinky.
- A growth spurt takes place.
- Axillary (underarm) hair appears.
- Marked voice changes take place.
- A beard develops.

It is helpful for children to know about these changes before they begin and later to be reassured, if they don't seem to be taking place at the same time as a friend's, that there *is* no *one* schedule for everyone's maturation. One pamphlet phrases an interchange on the subject this way:

"What's happening to me? I feel very strange and I don't know why."

"Your body is like a clock. At a certain time the pituitary gland (one of the ductless glands that is close to your brain) tells your sex gland—ovaries for girls, testicles for boys—to start working. They in turn tell the rest of your body to change. This message is sent all through your body by chemicals called hormones."

Besides reassuring boys and girls that the growth changes they are going through are normal, parents may want to add that it's perfectly okay if they feel ambivalent about growing up. It can be useful to talk about how they, the parents, felt at the same age and to point out current adolescent celebrities as examples of people undergoing noticeable changes, thus making the discussion less personal.

As with younger children, sometimes the questions do become much more personal. The following vignettes illustrate some common concerns of preteens and suggest ways in which parents might deal with them:

A mother and her eleven-year-old daughter were setting the table for Thanksgiving dinner when the daughter asked, "Mom, how old were you when you started getting your period?" Without stopping her folding of the napkins, the mother answered, "I was twelve, and my mother was fourteen when she got hers. It would be normal for you to start any time now."

A father going to bed very late one evening found his thirteen-year-old son dumping his sheets into the laundry hamper. The son muttered, "I'll bet this never happened to you." The father replied, "Wet dreams? Sure they did. I was so embarrassed I never told anyone. I thought I must be some kind of a freak because no one ever told me they're a normal part of growing up, being male and old enough to father a child. I still have them every now and then." He then helped his son get clean sheets and settle in for the night.

A twelve-year-old boy came out of the men's room in a filling station, climbed back into the car with his parents, and queried, "Were there rubbers when you were my age?" His mother replied, "There certainly were. I can remember boys carrying them around in their wallets and showing them off, like they were secrets." His father chuckled and replied, "Yes, I was one of those boys. I carried one around in my wallet all the way through high school—not a real wise move, since they rot with time. Now I know I should have replaced it if I didn't use it. Gee, I can't imagine me asking your granddad that question when I was your age!"

A father one of us knows reported that one Saturday, when he was driving his twelve-year-old daughter to a flute lesson, she asked, "Daddy, how old do you have to be to do it?" He took a deep breath and replied, "Well, it seems to me that having intercourse—that is what you mean, isn't it?—is a real special thing that you don't do just because you're old enough or because it feels good. The most important thing is to be very sure of your *own* feelings and not do it *because of* anyone else or *for* anyone else. Your mother and I don't believe kids your age are ready to handle it, but if you decide differently, it's important to avoid a pregnancy you wouldn't be able to manage by using birth control." (The chapter later in this book, "Talking About Values," contains a longer discussion of teenagers and intercourse.)

A dialogue like this last one gives parents an excellent opportunity to talk about their values. At Planned Parenthood we also believe there are strong health and developmental reasons for young people to abstain from intercourse. Some of these reasons include:

1. The very real risk of pregnancy and the complex decisions about the young couple's future that such an event entails. Research has shown that the younger teenagers are the first time they have intercourse, the less likely they are to use contraception.
2. The high risk of sexually transmissible diseases. STDs are being implicated in serious health problems, including sterility. Most young people want to have children at some time in the future and shouldn't risk losing that capacity.
3. The dangers of exploitation—for both young women and young men. The sex partner may be "using" the young person. When there is an age difference, this can be even more likely. Such exploitation can be damaging to the young person's later ability to develop into a trusting, caring adult.
4. There are indications that, even though girls mature physically at ages younger than boys, their emotional maturity may come later. Early first sexual experiences are often very unsatisfactory.
5. Doing *anything* simply because one's friends are doing it is never a good reason.

CHAPTER 7

The Top Seven Questions

Whenever boys and girls are asked in a sex education class about which aspects of sexuality they *most* want information, the following subjects are always at the top of their lists: menstruation, wet dreams, masturbation, intercourse and pregnancy, birth control, sexually transmitted diseases (STDs), and homosexuality. The regularity with which questions about these subjects are asked of educators is a clear sign that all young people, including teenagers who may already have had intercourse, can be woefully ignorant in areas that have a direct bearing on their health and emotional well-being. The information that follows is aimed at helping parents begin the conversations they need to have with their preteen and teenage children about the physiological and psychological aspects of sexual maturation.

MENSTRUATION

Even before the first sign of puberty, it is wise to talk about the changes that will start taking place, most importantly with regard to girls' menstruation.

The visible changes—in contours, height, skin—provide an

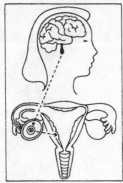

Menstruation

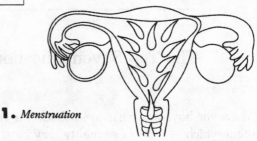

1. *Menstruation*

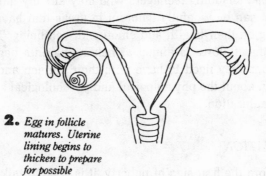

2. *Egg in follicle matures. Uterine lining begins to thicken to prepare for possible pregnancy.*

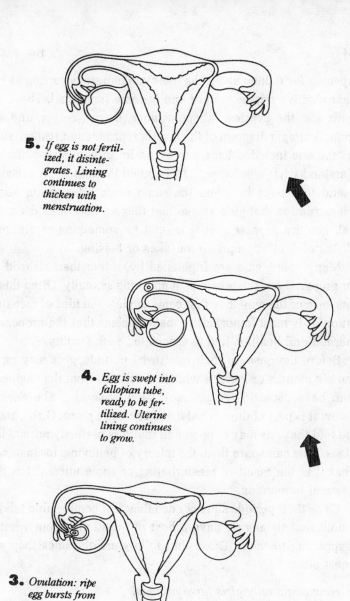

5. *If egg is not fertilized, it disintegrates. Lining continues to thicken with menstruation.*

4. *Egg is swept into fallopian tube, ready to be fertilized. Uterine lining continues to grow.*

3. *Ovulation: ripe egg bursts from ovary.*

opening for talking about the internal changes occurring as the reproductive organs mature and become functional. These organs are: the ovaries, fallopian tubes, uterus, cervix, and vagina. A simple diagram of the female reproductive system, such as the one included here, can be useful in helping a child understand what will happen. At Planned Parenthood we recommend that boys be given the same basic information about menstruation that girls are, so that they will see it as the natural, healthy process that it is—not as something mysterious, distasteful, or appropriate for jokes or teasing.

Many young girls are frightened by, rather than pleased by or prepared for, the prospect of maturing sexually. Often this is because of the way they first came to view the idea of menstruation. It is most important to make it clear that the process is normal and healthy, and is associated with fertility.

Before the onset of their menstrual periods, girls may have, for six months or more, a whitish discharge from the vagina. It can be substantial. A girl may be distressed if she doesn't know it is part of the normal changes taking place. Girls should be told that this may happen and that it is perfectly normal if it does. This can spare them the misery of believing, for instance, that it is the result of masturbating or some ailment too distasteful to mention.

Once their periods start or once they feel comfortable talking about that time, girls have a host of questions about what is happening to them. Those that follow are the ones they ask most often:

· *How come only girls have periods?*

Girls' hormones are different from boys'. Boys' hormones cause changes like voice deepening, facial hair, and ejaculation, along with growth. Girls' hormones cause the changes that make them able to have babies, and that includes the menstrual cycle along with the growth and development.

• *Does menstruation go on for the rest of your life?*

No. Usually until about age forty-five or fifty, when a woman's body stops secreting the female hormones that trigger it.

• *How long does a period last and how much blood is lost?*

The amount of discharge that flows out of the vagina and the length of time it takes both vary. For some girls the flow is only a few tablespoons of a fluid that starts out as brownish red, turns deep red and then lightens to rust color as it tapers off. Others may shed up to as much as half a cup or more over a period that can range from three days to a week. Only about four to six tablespoons of the flow is pure blood. The rest is extra bits of uterine lining that look like small, spongy clots. If the discharge is much more excessive than this and includes large clots of blood, it's wise to consult a doctor.

• *What is "regular," and is it normal not to be?*

The menstrual cycle is usually twenty-eight days, but there is no one normal length. Every woman's body has its own internal rhythm. When menstruation first starts, before the hormones get regulated, the length of the cycle may vary from month to month or may even skip a month. Irregularity is usually nothing to worry about, particularly in the first years. Getting sick or being worried or nervous can delay a period. As the body continues to mature, cycles and periods usually become more regular. Good health, a balanced diet, enough rest and exercise all play a part in regulating menstruation and minimizing any discomfort.

• *Is it better to use pads or tampons?*

That is a matter of individual preference. Contrary to what many people believe, most young girls who have not had intercourse can use tampons, though there may be difficulty with insertion the first few times. Once a girl has learned the knack of positioning a tampon correctly, she will not feel its presence. Many girls worry that a tampon can fall out or "get lost" inside their bodies. It cannot go up inside the body and rarely falls out (except occasionally when having a bowel movement). Even if the string gets drawn up inside the vagina, it can always be found. Whether tampons or pads are used, they should be changed several times a day to guard against odor or stains on clothes or growth of harmful bacteria. As a rule, no one else can tell whether a woman is menstruating.

· *What is toxic shock syndrome?*

This is a bacterial infection that is very rare but received a lot of publicity a few years ago. About one woman out of 25,000 using tampons may come down with it during her menstrual period. It starts in the vagina, probably due to an overgrowth of bacteria that are always there, and the toxin secreted by these bacteria gets into her bloodstream. Symptoms usually start with a sudden high fever, vomiting, and diarrhea. There may be a sunburnlike rash. It's imperative to remove the tampon immediately and get to a doctor. To cut down on the very slight risk of coming down with toxic shock syndrome, girls can use sanitary pads, at least at night.

· *What causes cramps?*

No one knows for sure, though there are many theories. Almost every woman has them at some time in her life, ranging from mild to severe. It may be some comfort for girls to know that cramps usually diminish as they grow older.

The usual remedies for cramps are a hot water bottle or heating pad on the abdomen and aspirin. Some people find that deep abdominal breathing and relaxation exercises help. If a girl has cramps severe enough to immobilize her every month, it would be wise to see a doctor.

· *What activities are okay during menstruation?*

Any activities that are okay at other times. Tennis, horseback riding, gym, exercise may help cramps. Showers, baths, swimming are perfectly fine and help girls feel fresher.

· *What is PMS?*

The cause of PMS (premenstrual syndrome), like cramps, is a

subject of much debate. Some believe it is caused by a hormone imbalance; others believe it is related to nutritional deficiencies or emotional problems.

The term "PMS" covers a wide range of emotional and physical changes that can take place during the seven to ten days before a menstrual period and that may be troublesome. These include pronounced mood swings, tension, anxiety or depression, lack of energy, bloating, backache, tenderness of the breasts, headaches, and vision disturbances, to name only some. Many women have at least several of the above symptoms before their periods, or what some might call "mild PMS." Getting plenty of rest and exercise, eating a balanced diet and cutting out sugar, coffee, and chocolate (even if there's a sudden craving for sweets) have helped many women. If symptoms are severe enough to warrant treatment, consult a physician specializing in gynecology. Many Planned Parenthood centers have information about PMS.

· *Can you get pregnant if you haven't started having your period?*

Yes. Ovulation usually occurs fourteen days prior to a period. That means you're able to get pregnant before your first period.

· *Are there other reasons besides pregnancy for periods to stop, or be late or scanty?*

Girls who engage in regular, *strenuous* physical activity, like ballet dancing, distance running, or gymnastics, may be late in starting to menstruate. Or if the exercise is begun after periods have been established, their periods may stop or occur infrequently. This is called amenorrhea. Anorexia is another possible cause of missed periods. Normal periods usually resume if the exercise is decreased or the anorexic's starvation regime is halted.

Occasionally illness (most often chronic disease) may cause periods to be missed or scanty. Quite rarely stress or depression can cause menstrual irregularities.

To pinpoint the reason, a parent might ask whether this has

happened before and, if not, whether the girl is certain she's late. Variations in cycle between twenty-one and thirty-five days are within the normal range.

If there is the slightest possibility that a missed period might be caused by pregnancy, seek professional help right away. Nowadays highly sensitive tests can detect the hormones of pregnancy within five to seven days after a missed period. It is also possible to have a scanty period early in a pregnancy.

How to Help Your Daughter Be Prepared For Menstruation

There are simple, practical steps parents can take to ensure that their daughters don't find their first experience of menstruation disturbing or embarrassing. To an adult, they may seem obvious, but a young girl for whom this is a momentous change will appreciate all the help she can get. We suggest:

- After you have explained the biology of menstruation to your daughter and answered her questions about it, help her prepare by providing whatever supplies you jointly decide are most practical. You might shop when she is with you to help her develop self-confidence about acquiring them for herself.
- Make sure she understands how to use the pads or tampons and how to dispose of them. Talk about what she should do if her first period starts while she is in school or away from home. There are probably vending machines in the girls' bathroom that sell pads and tampons. If not, the school nurse or a friend may be of help.
- If she is among the first or the last in her peer group to menstruate, reassure her that everyone matures at her own rate.
- Remind her that she'll feel fresher and worry less about unpleasant odors if she changes a pad or tampon several times a day and showers once a day or more.

Remember that all this is new for your daughter and that your matter-of-fact and reassuring words are what will make it seem the normal experience it should be.

THE BIG CHANGES FOR BOYS

Boys usually become sexually mature somewhat later than girls. Girls can show the first signs of puberty as young as nine. For boys it is more likely to be around eleven. Thus the growth spurt that girls go through at around age twelve will not occur for boys until they are around fourteen. Lagging behind girls in this way, plus the tremendously wide variation in growth patterns among males, can make growing comfortable in their new bodies a tough job for many boys.

Most parents are aware that they should discuss menstruation with their daughters. Boys deserve equal time for their concerns of early puberty. The discussions, we think, can be done in the same way as discussions with daughters about menstruation. Commenting on a son's growth and change gives parents an opportunity to begin an explanation of wet dreams and of the other topics discussed below. If parents keep firmly in mind the goal of helping their children understand their bodies, the mechanics of achieving that goal will seem less important. For instance, a boy should not only know what ejaculation is, but understand that he is now capable of impregnating a girl.

Just as menstruation is the most dramatic evidence of maturing for girls, a boy's ability to ejaculate semen in early adolescence is a sign that he is becoming a man. Although he has been able to have erections since birth (even when he was in the uterus), it is not until the male hormone, testosterone, begins to be released into the bloodstream that the testes are able to make sperm.

What happens then can be dismaying to boys if they are not prepared for it. Many of them learn of their new ability to ejaculate while masturbating, but sometimes they have their first experience of it in a nocturnal emission or "wet dream." If they haven't been told that this may happen, it can be at the worst frightening—"Do I have a venereal disease?"—and at the least

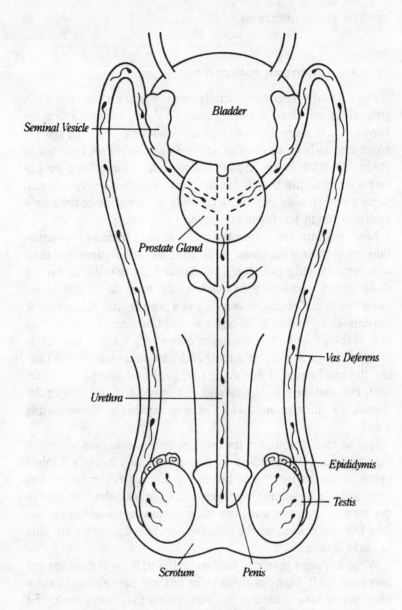

Bladder

Seminal Vesicle

Prostate Gland

Urethra

Vas Deferens

Epididymis

Testis

Scrotum

Penis

embarrassing—"Did I wet the bed? What'll I do about the sheets?" If they are told before the first such happening that this is a normal event, one they needn't feel embarrassed about, boys can relax rather than be upset by their harmless wet dreams.

Help for parents trying to talk about sexuality can come from unexpected quarters, as the following anecdote told to us by a mother points out. Her seventh-grade daughter suddenly piped up at the dinner table, "What's a wet dream?" The mother looked expectantly to the father for a reply, only to see him gaze fixedly at his plate, so she said, "We'll talk about it later." Her sixteen-year-old son looked up and said, "I think we ought to talk about it now." As a result, the mother told us, they had the best family discussion they'd ever had on an aspect of sexual functioning.

Another phenomenon of male adolescence that boys come to worry about is their frequent, involuntary erections. Adult males looking back on their teens usually ruefully recall these as invariably happening when they were called on in class, when they were in the car with their grandmothers, or when they were passing the plate in church. It is a kindness to reassure sons that they are not alone in this phenomenon, that it is not abnormal or a sign of being perverted or oversexed, any more than their sexual fantasies or surges of sexual desire are, and that the frequency of these spontaneous erections will diminish with time. Parents might want to add that blood flow throughout the body increases when we are relaxed and feeling good. This is one cause of erection for boys.

Sex role stereotyping causes pubertal boys just as much confusion and anxiety about their changing selves as it does girls, but it also dictates that they aren't supposed to admit it, thereby adding to their misery. Because masculinity and, by implication, sexual adequacy have traditionally been associated with size and strength, the boy who is slow to grow or slight of build is often made to feel like a total misfit. Being just like everyone else is as desperate a need for boys as it is for girls. While one boy dreads changing clothes in the boys' locker room because he hasn't yet developed pubic hair, another boy is frantically shaving it off because he is the only one in his locker room who has. Teenage boys need to be able to talk to their parents about the things that worry them fully as much as girls do.

It is safe to say that one thing that is guaranteed to worry boys at some point in their development is penis size. One reason is that it usually "feels adult" (i.e., is sensitive to stimulation) considerably earlier than it assumes an adult appearance—in middle or late adolescence. Again, etched into the memories of every adult male are the locker room comparisons of penis size that were either a source of triumph or humiliation.

It's reassuring to young teenage boys for parents to explain the wide variations in growth rate and to explain, as well, that the size of an erect penis is not related to its size when it is not. Most adult men's penises, no matter what size they are when they are flaccid, measure around four to six inches when erect. This is also a good time to make sure boys have an accurate understanding of female physiological structure and realize that nature intended penises and vaginas to accommodate to one another.

As though adolescence wasn't difficult enough for boys, about 60 to 70 percent of them suffer through a temporary swelling of breasts during its early years (twelve to fourteen). The enlargement may appear as a definite tender mass, usually under the nipple on one or both sides. It may or may not be noticeable to other people. If it is, it can cause a young boy anxiety. In any case, if it doesn't subside within a year or eighteen months, it should be checked by a doctor to make sure it isn't one of the rare cases of this condition caused by disease or an endocrine disorder.

MASTURBATION

Down through the ages, one of society's strongest prohibitions has been against masturbation. Nonetheless, estimates are that over 90 percent of men and women have masturbated by the age of twenty-one. But because of the ancient prohibitions (now generally discredited), it is an experience so guilt-connected for most adults that they find it very difficult to discuss openly.

Parents particularly can have strongly conflicting feelings about it. Unless they're unusually unobservant, they are almost certain to be confronted at some point with evidence of their children's masturbatory activities. If they accept both intellectually and emotionally the fact that masturbation is a natural and harmless expression of sexuality—and can also accept the fact that a child is a sexual being—they can usually handle the situation calmly and nonjudgmentally. On the other hand, if, like many adults today, they accept the modern view of masturbation intellectually but are still emotionally influenced by the stern injunctions against it with which they grew up, they may find themselves saying one thing and acting out another. "Yes" becomes "no" when it is said with a frown.

As we mentioned in Part I, many babies begin to explore their genitals in a haphazard fashion almost from birth. And, finding it pleasant, they continue to do so in a more purposeful way off and on for the rest of their lives. So the first time parents may be confronted with evidence of their children's sexuality is while they are still very young. This is the time to determine an attitude toward masturbation with which they feel comfortable. Determining that now will make communication a lot more relaxed later, when emotions too often gain the upper hand, yet words are still important.

Today all the old myths about the evils and dangers of masturbation have been totally discredited by scientific research. Even many church groups have modified their stand, seeing it more as a healthy, normal release of sexual tension than as the sinful, unnatural act it was once considered to be. Perhaps by the time today's babies are grown up, everyone will be able to view it without guilt as just one of many sexual options.

Meanwhile, what is today's parent to do? Our advice, the first time you see a small child fondling himself, is to take this teachable moment and try to get across the message that masturbating is something practically everyone does because it feels good, that there's nothing wrong with it, that it's okay with you (if it is), but that it is something to be done in private. Even a four-year-old can understand this message. No one can completely stop a child from ever masturbating. Parental disapproval simply increases the likelihood that worry, guilt, and anxiety will become associated with masturbation.

Many parents who accept masturbation as all right, worry nevertheless that a child might be "doing it too much." According to experts, there is no such thing as "too much" if a child is emotionally and psychologically healthy. On the other hand, a child who masturbates publicly or compulsively may have problems that need professional attention.

Masturbation takes on new importance for children when they enter puberty and begin to feel a newly urgent sex drive. It can also become one more thing about which to worry unnecessarily and endlessly, one more guilt-provoking need to satisfy. Although much discussed, it is also, very likely, a subject they can't get reassurance about from their friends.

Adolescent boys and girls would both welcome reassurance from their parents—people whose values they trust—that solitary sexual activity is okay. They would be even more relieved to hear that it actually has undeniable benefits. Those that are mentioned most often by educators and sex therapists are:

- It allows young children to learn about their bodies.
- It relieves sexual tension and reduces the pressure to become prematurely involved in sexual activity with another person.

- It can teach young males how to delay ejaculation so that as adults they can be better sex partners. Fear of discovery may result in a desire to ejaculate quickly rather than to prolong the pleasure/danger.
- It teaches girls what arouses them and what leads to orgasm, making it more likely that they will have better sexual experiences as adults.

Girls are usually secretive about masturbating. But many boys, at some point in their development, make it a group event with one or more boys. Later these masturbatory encounters can become a source of guilt and anxiety if they are believed to be early indications of homosexuality. Adolescent boys need to be reassured that homosexual sex play or fantasies do not mean this is a permanent orientation. (See the section on homosexuality.) Your child may have no questions about masturbation, but questions about other topics, such as virginity or physiology, may really be disguised questions on the subject. For example, these are some questions we have heard and some suggested responses.

Q. "Is having intercourse the only way to not be a virgin?"
A. Yes, that is the meaning of the word. A virgin is a person who has not had intercourse. Masturbation is not the same as intercourse. Masturbating is perfectly normal—most people have tried it.
Q. "Is it wrong to play with yourself? I think it means that the person is ready to have sex but is chicken."
A. "In my view, it's not wrong to 'play with yourself' or masturbate. Many people, men and women, masturbate occasionally throughout their lives—and other people, for whom the idea is unpleasant, never masturbate at all. Some people think masturbation is wrong."
Q. "Can a guy use up all his sperm?"
A. No, it's continually being produced in the testicles. So wet dreams or masturbation can't use up all the sperm. They are

both normal behaviors for people your age. Intercourse doesn't use up all a man's sperm either.

Q. "If somebody puts her finger in her vagina, will it break her hymen?"

A. If a girl has a hymen, putting her finger in her vagina might break it or it might simply stretch the opening in it. Some girls do not have this membrane across the opening to the vagina. For those who do, it generally stretches and disappears as the young woman matures. Masturbation or self-exploration isn't harmful to it.

Sometimes words may be mentioned that will provide a "teachable moment." For instance, if you are with your child and you hear "jerk off" used in a negative comment about someone, ask if the child knows what the phrase means and explain that it's another word for masturbation. Then you might want to discuss how "jerk off" is used to give a bad or negative connotation to something—masturbation—which is not itself bad or damaging.

In the context of talking about maturing, about menstruation, about sex, include discussions of masturbation. It is a normal activity that most people have tried, one that some people continue throughout their lives. You might want to be prepared with your own answer when your child then asks you if you masturbate. You may decide that you will say, "This is very personal, and I am uncomfortable telling you about my sex life." On the other hand, if parents can share the feelings they experienced as youngsters, it can relieve the child's anxiety.

Talking about masturbation can be difficult. If, even with the assistance of this book, you feel uncomfortable, there are other options—such as telling your child that you are unsure of yourself on this subject, but that you know there is a good book such as this one, which has helpful information. You and your child might benefit from reading it together.

INTERCOURSE AND PREGNANCY

A recent TV talk show about sex education included a group of high school students on its panel. A thoughtful-looking boy, probably around sixteen, made this memorable statement: "Fear is the most common feeling people our age have about sex."

There are no statistics available to back up that comment, but it has the ring of truth. To the uninitiated, the concept of sexual intercourse can't help but produce fear on a number of levels. Its implications are awesome.

Next to fear, the overriding emotion of those who have not experienced sex is curiosity. How, exactly, is intercourse performed? Every teenager wonders at some point. How can people find out if they are "doing it" correctly? How often do most people have intercourse? What does an orgasm feel like? On the same show just mentioned, a teenage boy in the audience asked solemnly, "Is losing your virginity a requirement for maturity?"

The primarily erotic aspects of human sexuality are the most difficult ones for the majority of parents and children to discuss, but youngsters deserve more accurate information than they can get from each other. If family communication about the less emotionally charged sexual topics has been relatively easy through the years, it can probably be maintained on this new level after puberty. A good ground rule for both sides to accept is the right not to talk about any particular matter on too personal a level.

However, if it seems truly impossible for a mother or father to give pubertal or adolescent children the sexual information they will need for their own protection, he or she should find a substitute. Possibilities include the other parent, a minister or rabbi, a doctor, or a teacher of sex education. Quite often adolescents feel more comfortable talking with their friends' parents than with their own. If natural parents have no objections,

such people are possible substitutes. Many parents feel unnecessarily hurt or rejected, though, if their children turn to others
with questions. It is rarely intended as a rejection, and parents
should rejoice if their teenagers have found a reliable source of
information.

One of the advantages of not delaying conversation with
most ten- to twelve-year-olds about the more "grown-up" aspects of sexuality is that at this age they can usually still be
discussed more impersonally and less emotionally than will be
possible later on.

By puberty, around age twelve, most young people are mature enough to understand fully the mechanics of reproduction
for the first time. They are becoming interested, as well, in
male and female social and sexual relationships and the
broader implications of sexuality—but without yet being
deeply involved. The climate is right to talk about such things
as why some teenagers choose to have sexual relations or risk
pregnancy, about the responsibilities these relationships entail,
and about the rules and standards each family expects its teenagers to observe. Talking these matters out before they become
controversial will help keep parent-child relationships below
the boiling point later on.

It is also a good time to provide the information that older
teenagers will desperately want but may be afraid to ask for by
the time it might apply to them.

A girl will want to know whether intercourse hurts very
much the first time and whether a penis, seemingly so much
larger than her vagina, can injure her. She should know that a
virgin's first experience may be painful but is unlikely to cause
injury. She should also know that girls rarely have an orgasm
the first time they have intercourse. In fact, the rather sparse
information available on the subject suggests that early intercourse experiences are disappointing to most teenagers.

A fifteen-year-old young woman who was a member of a
teen panel talking to educators told us, "My mother says that
intercourse is overrated."

The main worry boys have is usually about their performance. Nervousness and inexperience may make it difficult for
them to achieve and maintain an erection, a problem, they
might be reassured, which is usually overcome.

Even if teenagers begin sexual relations before their parents
feel they should, they deserve to know that they are not frigid
or failures if they have worries about performance. They deserve to be told that enjoyment of sex takes time and experience, and that it is too bad society presents it as more of a
competitive sport than an expression of love.

The questions boys and girls have about pregnancy, once it
can happen to or be caused by them, are very different from
those they had when they were younger and had only an impersonal curiosity in the subject.

Because the possibility of becoming pregnant is frightening
to most young people, "magical thinking" is likely to take over.
Magical thinking is what causes such myths as "you can't get
pregnant the first time you have sex"; "you can't get pregnant if
you have it standing up"; or "if you've been having sex for
three months without a pregnancy resulting, it is not going to
happen."

In adolescence such matters as menstruation, sexual relations, pregnancy, and childbirth, which earlier seemed almost
unrelated, all come together and take on newly urgent interest.
It is a good time to reinforce the idea of cause and effect and to
remind both boys and girls how the menstrual cycle works and
how unintended pregnancies come about. If they are not already doing so, girls might be encouraged to keep a chart of
their cycle, if only to pinpoint irregularity or the occurrence of
menstrual difficulties.

It is also an opportunity to talk about why adults choose to
have babies and the responsibilities that having them entails.
Most Americans expect to become parents "sooner or later,"
and most expect to have two children. Some of the considerations people have when they think about becoming parents
include: the joys of seeing a baby grow; the closeness of the

family; worry about being a "good" parent; the cost of raising a child (now estimated to be over $100,000 for the child's first seventeen years); the necessity of child care if the mother wants to, or must, work; and the responsibility of being so important in another person's life.

"How can a girl tell if she's pregnant?" is a question that preoccupies many teenagers. The answer is that she can't for certain, but she can suspect she is if she has been involved in sexual activity and has missed one or more periods. Among other common symptoms are swollen and tender breasts, nausea (particularly in the morning), increased vaginal secretions, fatigue, bowel irregularities, and a tendency to urinate more often. A number of tests can answer the question with certainty. If she doesn't feel she can talk to either of her parents about her worry, she should visit a doctor or a Planned Parenthood center. They can give her the information and help she needs and will respect her confidentiality. Trying to deny a pregnancy has never made it go away.

Teenagers should also know that it is possible to get pregnant from intercourse even when experiencing some menstruation-like bleeding and that it is possible to get pregnant even if the male withdraws before ejaculation. Some fluid comes out of the penis before ejaculation and can contain sperm. If the boy ejaculates near the entrance to the girl's vagina, it's possible for the sperm to get into the vagina and make her pregnant. This is the explanation for the rare but occasional occurrence of a "pregnant virgin."

Other questions commonly asked in school sex education classes and the kinds of answers usually given include:

"Alice told me you can't get pregnant if you have sex standing up. Is that true?"

"No, it's not, though a lot of teens and even some grown-ups might believe it. Girls can get pregnant any time they have sex, even the first time, if they don't use birth control."

"How come it's okay for adults who aren't married to have sex, but not for kids?"

"Some people believe that sex is only for married people. Others believe that adults are more in charge of their lives than teenagers still living with their parents are and are better able to deal with the emotional parts of a relationship which includes sex. They are also more likely to use birth control so the woman doesn't get pregnant by mistake. Generally adults are less likely to have sex to "prove" something like being adult or independent or "in love.""

"Sex on TV always seems so great. Is it really like that?"

"Sex isn't always great—not even for married people who are very much in love. TV seldom deals with the realities of everyday living. People have to learn about loving each other, and that includes sexual love.""

"How old do you have to be to get pregnant or to get a girl pregnant?"

"A boy has to be able to ejaculate. A girl can get pregnant as soon as she has ovulated. The age at which this happens can vary from person to person. Sometimes a girl ovulates even before she begins having periods. This means she can become pregnant.""

Anyone who has successfully negotiated the maze that sex represents for young people today, who understands how frightened and anxious most of them are, must surely feel compelled to give them all the help possible in understanding it.

BIRTH CONTROL

"My child isn't interested in boys, why should I talk to her about birth control?" "If I talk to him about contraception, he'll believe I think it's okay to have sex." These are comments we at Planned Parenthood hear over and over again. Some parents believe that avoiding such discussions is the most loving thing they can do for their child. However, there is no indication that parents' talking about sexual behavior with their children encourages them to experiment with sex. Instead, there is strong evidence that both boys and girls who feel free to talk to their parents about birth control are more likely to be responsible about its use when they do have sex than those who do not discuss it.

In this country, many teenagers do not use birth control at all or use it inconsistently. One reason for this is that sexually active teens often feel guilty about what they are doing. They feel even more guilty if they admit to themselves that their behavior is premeditated. So they try to convince themselves that they did not or are not planning to have sex and when they do it is because they are swept away by uncontrollable passion. Using birth control would give the lie to this argument. "Magical thinking" of this kind, which unfortunately is widespread, is less appealing to teenagers who feel able to talk realistically with their parents about the need for responsible planning.

At Planned Parenthood, we believe the best time to give information about birth control is *before* boys and girls might relate it to themselves. This decreases the possibility of confusing information with permission. It also makes it possible for parents to say non-accusingly, "We hope very much that *you* won't get sexually involved until you're mature enough to handle it, but if you ever decide to, please use one of the kinds of birth control we told you about." Once this has been said, teenagers know they need not be afraid that buying or using contraceptives is going to bring on parental wrath.

In 1982 the Survey of Family Growth, done by the U.S. Department of Health and Human Services, found that 68 percent of unmarried young women 15 to 19 who had had intercourse had used contraception the last time they had intercourse. The *first* time these unmarried young women had had intercourse, over half of them had used NO contraception. A similar study in 1979 found that a quarter of unmarried, sexually active young women said they NEVER used contraception. The result is an epidemic in this country of unintended pregnancies which too often end tragically for the young parents or for the child. Health professionals have done extensive research to uncover the reasons for the high number of teen pregnancies and births, and they agree that the following are the most common:

- Ignorance, misunderstanding, misinformation—all of which contribute to the non-use of contraceptives. Myths such as "the pill causes cancer" or "I'm too young to get pregnant" abound in this age group.
- Many teens mistakenly believe that contraceptive devices are difficult to obtain, costly, or require parental permission to buy.
- Magical thinking—"It'll never happen to me"—and guilt feelings about sexual behavior. (These are very common.)
- The sporadic nature of most teenage intercourse and the fact that it really is often spontaneous.

Contrary to what many adults believe, the "sexually active" adolescent may have intercourse no more than once—but once is enough to get pregnant—or as infrequently as two or three times in a year—not often enough to make using contraception a habit.

Research by Planned Parenthood shows that the average girl has been sexually active for six months before she uses a contraceptive and for eleven months before she comes to a family planning clinic. It has also been determined that her partner's attitude about contraception plays an important role in her decision to use it. Most teenagers, male and female, say they believe in showing responsibility about the use of birth control, but many fewer actually do so. The inconsistency between what they say and what they do doesn't surprise professionals familiar with this age group. Teenagers are still working to establish their identities and are easily swayed by all kinds of influences. They need all the positive reinforcement they can get to translate responsible attitudes into responsible behavior.

A double standard still prevails about responsibility for pregnancy prevention. Particularly since the advent of the pill, many boys assume girls will take care of contraception.

When parents talk to their children about birth control they would do well to make them aware of these reasons many teens do not use birth control. Most adults would agree that these are unacceptable reasons for avoiding the use of contraception. They can tell them at the same time that all the following statements are UNTRUE:

· Swallowing a birth control pill before or after intercourse prevents pregnancy.
· A girl can't get pregnant if she only started menstruating recently.
· Saran Wrap can be successfully substituted for a condom.
· A girl can't get pregnant if she doesn't have an orgasm.
· It is illegal for minors to buy nonprescription contraceptives.
· Taking a douche after intercourse or squirting a carbonated drink into the vagina will prevent pregnancy.
· Condoms are unreliable because they break easily.
· Parents are automatically notified if minors visit a family planning clinic.
· It is not necessary to use birth control if you only have sex occasionally.
· Birth control is the girl's responsibility.
· Withdrawal is the best method of birth control for young people.
· The IUD has to be put in every time a couple has sex.
· Everybody else is "doing it."

There are presently at least seven accepted methods of birth control available for men and women. Pamphlets describing them in detail are available at all Planned Parenthood centers and other family planning centers.

The methods of contraception, listed in order from generally most effective to generally least effective, are: the pill; the IUD; the barrier methods of condom or diaphragm, contraceptive sponge; spermicides; withdrawal and the fertility awareness methods, such as calendar rhythm, basal body temperature monitoring and cervical mucous examination, which require periodic abstinence. The pill, the IUD,* and the diaphragm require a visit to a doctor or clinic. Each method has distinct advantages and disadvantages which should be explained before a possible user makes a decision. (See the appendices at the end of this book.)

A highly satisfactory method for teenagers, who generally do not have intercourse frequently, is a combination of nonprescription contraceptives, such as foam or sponge for the female and a condom for the male. Such combinations are recommended because they are effective, inexpensive, easily available in almost any drugstore, and not complicated to use. The drawback is that, since they must be used *at* the time of intercourse, a teenage couple who is "swept away" may be unable or unwilling to stop and protect themselves every time. We recommend that young people consult a health professional as to what method of birth control is best for them.

Some parents hesitate to provide reinforcement about the use of contraception because they are really opposed to their teenagers having intercourse at all. Some teenagers can be considerably offended if a parent mentions contraception to them, "like, she just assumes I'm having sex," as one fifteen-year-old who was not having sex put it. No doubt about it, it's a complex issue.

At Planned Parenthood we believe that an important part of providing the familial structure and control adolescents need in their lives is to let them know how parents feel about teenage and premarital sex—and why. We also recognize that parental control lessens as children grow. Reliable statistics show that over half of today's teenagers will have had intercourse by the time they finish high school. So we strongly urge parents to tell their teenagers that if they choose to have intercourse, knowing the family attitude about it, the parents want them to have access to contraception.

Some parents may choose to give the child information about

* Note: The IUD may no longer be available in the United States.

contraception, some may choose to tell the teenager where they can get contraception, and some may make an appointment for the young person with a local physician or clinic. The dynamics of the approach will, of course, vary with the teenager and the parent. Indeed, some mothers bring in daughters who decline to accept contraception. At one Planned Parenthood center, a mother brought her daughter in, but the daughter paid for her own contraceptives, since the decision to have intercourse was hers. Another mother bought some contraceptive sponges at the drugstore and left them in her teenager's bathroom.

In 1985, The Alan Guttmacher Institute conducted a study of teenage sexual behavior and teenage pregnancy, done in six developed countries, where the proportion of teenagers who have had intercourse is similar to that of the United States. The study found that not one of these countries had teen pregnancy or abortion or birth rates anywhere as high as those in the United States. For example, in Sweden, long described as a sexually permissive society, teen pregnancy rates are less than half those in the U.S.; and in the Netherlands, where the same numbers of teens seem to have intercourse as in the U.S., the pregnancy rate is only one seventh that of ours.

What are they doing differently in Sweden, the Netherlands, Canada, England, and Scotland? The researchers conclude that governmental policy in these five countries seems to be to stop teen pregnancy rather than to stop teen sex. So they are very direct in their approach to contraception. It is accessible and usually at no cost for teenagers. Explicit information about sexuality and contraception is widely available and is accepted as an integral part of young people's education. Although the report talks about countries rather than individual families, we believe it holds equally true on a family level. If parents do not want their children to become pregnant or to make someone pregnant while they are teenagers, they must give them information about contraception and, by so doing, give them permission to use it when they have sex. Otherwise, parental silence may result in an unintended pregnancy. Generally speaking, this is a dilemma most parents want to avoid.

SEXUALLY TRANSMISSIBLE DISEASES (STDs)

The teenage world abounds with scare stories about sexually transmissible diseases—a term that includes what used to be called venereal disease—but it is disastrously lacking in accurate information that might protect boys and girls from one of the major health problems of their age group. Thanks to the media, genital herpes and AIDS are known to almost everyone. Fewer people realize that gonorrhea and chlamydial infections are at epidemic proportions in the United States or that roughly two thirds of the cases involve young people between the ages of fifteen and twenty-four. No one can afford to be ignorant about STDs today.

Sexually active teenagers are particularly vulnerable to STDs and their complications for unique reasons that make it especially important to warn them of the dangers. Even if teenagers know there are such things as STDs, they are often not psychologically mature enough to accept the fact that they themselves might need protection. "If you don't think about it, it won't happen" is often the operating principle with adolescents. They may be too embarrassed to buy contraceptives, several of which offer some protection from STDs, and may be even more reluctant to seek health information or care. Frequently they are not comfortable enough with a sexual partner to talk frankly about something like STDs, thus possibly helping to perpetuate and spread them. And, finally, there are so many changes taking place in their bodies that they may not recognize symptoms for what they are.

The best protection parents can offer their children is to make sure they know the facts before they become sexually active. If they make it clear then that the subject will always be open for discussion just like any other illness children might contract, their offspring will be more likely to confide in them if they later need help.

These are the most important facts for boys and girls to know:

- Adolescents are at high risk of contracting STDs for the reasons outlined above. And STDs are frighteningly widespread in this country. Gonorrhea is known to affect one million Americans every year. Unreported cases could bring the number of sufferers up to eight million. As many as twenty million Americans are believed to suffer from genital herpes.
- It is easier to avoid contracting an STD than it is to cure it. Symptoms can be hard to detect until the disease has been harbored long enough to cause complications and possibly to infect numerous others. Chlamydia and gonorrhea are two examples of STD that can be present without symptoms.
- Some STDs can be extremely serious, even life-threatening. Gonorrhea can have serious complications, including pelvic inflammatory disease (PID), which is estimated to have resulted in sterility for up to 18,000 girls between the ages of fifteen and nineteen. According to the *Journal of Adolescent Health Care*, one out of every eight sexually active sixteen-year-old girls develops PID. In men and boys it can cause narrowing or blocking of the urethra, difficulty in getting an erection, and sterility.
- It is possible, but infrequent, for a child or teenager to get AIDS. The percentage of children with the disease is 1 percent of all cases. Teenagers account for less than 1 percent. Children can get AIDS from a mother who has it or from transfusions of blood that contain the AIDS virus.

Doctors are quite certain that the only way to transmit AIDS sexually is through intimate contact with the bodily fluids of someone who has the disease. Although new information is coming out all the time, saliva exchanged from kissing is still considered an unlikely vehicle for transmitting

AIDS. And casual or household contact is not known to have caused any cases.

- It is *easy* to get confidential medical treatment for STDs. It is often free or based on ability to pay. A minor does not need parental consent for treatment, and it is important to get treatment as early as possible. A leaflet available at Planned Parenthood affiliates lists a number of resources.
- Using a condom gives effective protection against STDs to both partners. Diaphragms and vaginal contraceptives offer some, but not as much, protection to females.
- Urinating right after intercourse and washing genitals thoroughly with soap and water can lessen the risk of infection. This is particularly true of syphilis.
- Several STDs can be contracted *without having intercourse.* Pharyngeal gonorrhea can be spread from infected male or female genitals to the pharynx, the region between mouth and throat. Herpes and syphilis can also be spread through oral sex.
- Having had an STD does not confer immunity. Reinfection can occur. It is also quite common to have more than one STD at a time.
- A youngster who has not been sexually active need not worry that he or she has an STD. So much misinformation abounds that teens sometimes worry needlessly if they have any kind of genital problem and are too embarrassed to ask for help.
- Symptoms that the sexually active person should have checked out by a doctor include:

  painful, burning, or dark-colored urine

  discharges from the vagina or penis that itch, burn, or have an unusual odor

  persistent sore throat

  soreness, redness, sores, warts, or a persistent pimple in the genital area.

Physicians who treat teenagers are particularly concerned about the rising incidence of chlamydia and/or gonorrhea in this age group and the difficulties associated with diagnosing and treating them. Control of the disease through treatment of sexual partners is made difficult by the fact that most teenagers are reluctant to identify their partners to a doctor. Many adolescents are so hurt and angry at learning they have been infected that they find it impossible to discuss, even with the person responsible.

The social stigma attached to STDs that has made them "unmentionable" gives parents an important motive for making sure their children are aware both of the dangers and of how to protect themselves. Young people need to know that using condoms, and even creams and jellies, significantly reduces the risk of contracting most diseases; they should understand the importance of good hygiene for themselves and their partners; and they should be able to recognize the early warning signs of STDs. The descriptions in the appendix can be useful for this.

HOMOSEXUALITY

As much as 8 percent of the population is primarily involved in sexual and love relationships with persons of the same sex. The chances are, then, that we all have homosexual or lesbian relatives, friends, or acquaintances. Still, discussions about lesbianism and homosexuality evoke a wide range of feelings that are often complicated. The most positive approach to this subject is to remember that same-sex relationships may be equal to heterosexual relationships in their capacity for loving and caring.

For young children there is no point in detailing the complexities or physiological aspects of same-sex relationships. But seven- or eight-year-olds may be puzzled when they hear references to homosexuality or lesbianism. They will need guidance to avoid developing prejudices, which could become burdens later on, when they have urgent questions about their own sexual identities. Helpful discussion of sexual identity will always be possible if an honest background for talking about the subject has been established.

For many children, the first words they hear about homosexuality are derogatory. Words like "fag," "queer," "pansy," and "lesbo" are repeated by children who have only a hazy notion, if any, of what is meant. These words are used in anger, to tease, or to ridicule. Children easily understand how language can be hurtful and it is easy to point out how cruel these words can be. If the child knows homosexual men or lesbian women as friends, it is even simpler. "These words are used to hurt people's feelings—people like Jon and Jim, for instance, who have special friendships with people of the same sex." For a young child that may be all that is needed. It may be pointed out at such a time that "Jon and Jim" describe themselves as "gay."

Teenagers reflect society's increasingly liberalized attitudes toward homosexuality and lesbianism. Many recognize that neither is considered an illness or psychosis by health and social work professionals. Many know that the factors that determine the sexual direction of a person's life are yet to be fully understood and that sexual identity is not something chosen or easily changed. But for all of this sophistication, teenagers' anxieties about their sexual identities are often painful. They may fear that a sexual experience they have had or a sexual fantasy they have enjoyed about someone of the same gender is proof of homosexuality. Consequently, with puberty, all sorts of questions may arise. How can you tell if someone is homosexual? Does masturbating mean you're one? Does a lisp mean you're one? Is it possible to be both male and female? Is homosexuality a perversion?

In our society, which puts such a premium on archetypal qualities of "masculinity" and "femininity," it is no wonder that boys and girls might suffer from doubts about their sexual identity. Those who are late in developing, those who haven't a very strong sex drive, boys and girls who are virgins—even if only for lack of opportunity—may all believe they are fated for homosexuality. Almost all of them can be honestly assured that this is not the case.

Girls and boys need especially to be reassured that sexual play with a friend of one's own gender is fairly common and that it is not an indication of future, adult homosexuality. This is a frequent and secret worry of many young people—particularly boys. Boys and girls should also know that having "a crush" on someone of the same sex is not an indication of homosexual preference. In fact, it is a very normal part of growing up—a step from the self-centeredness of childhood to the emotional interaction with others of adulthood. If a child is encouraged to talk about a crush it may lose some of its intensity. In any case, it is unlikely to last forever.

For young people who realize they are truly homosexual in their preferences, the greatest difficulty is admitting it—to themselves as well as to others. It's hard for adults who must cope with experiences of isolation, discrimination, or rejection. For adolescents, who crave acceptance above almost everything, it can be an agony. Tolerance is often lacking in teenagers. Adolescents who are "straight" (heterosexually oriented) are likely to react negatively. They fear guilt by association. They may become more tolerant as they get older, but most young heterosexuals find other sexual preferences difficult to understand, and their prejudices add to the burdens of their gay peers.

Telling parents is often what young lesbians and homosexuals dread most. The fear of parental rejection, and of being the cause of grief to those loved as deeply as parents, often leads a gay teenager toward a painful secrecy that can last a lifetime. For most parents of lesbian or homosexual children the road to acceptance is difficult. They are likely to have little information or understanding of homosexuality and to be deeply disturbed by what they see as the "waste" of their son's or daughter's life as a result of homosexuality. Homosexuality may also violate their religious beliefs, and, though needless, parents often feel great guilt for having failed somehow in their parenting. They may even feel their own sexual adequacy threatened by the revelation. One mother, who eventually was able to come to terms with the situation, has said that at first she felt a "great overwhelming loss . . . a helpless, hopeless feeling that was to remain with me for months—almost as if the Ron we knew had died."

With the help of a pastoral counselor, she and her husband were able to see the uselessness of looking for causes—because no one really knows what they are. They were able to stop blaming themselves and to keep open the lines of communication with their son. These are probably the most important things parents can do if they want to preserve their relationship with a child struggling with the real necessity to differ from what society considers a normal lifestyle. Such children need all the support and understanding parents can give. Mothers and fathers who need help themselves in order to deal with their feelings or behavior may find it useful to get in touch with an organization like The National Federation of Parents and Friends of Lesbians and Gays, P.O. Box 24565, Los Angeles, CA 90024.

A piece of practical advice that many counselors give young people who know or believe they are homosexual is not to be too anxious to make it widely public. Not only is a person's sexual preference not the world's business, but it may change, and "coming out" is a choice that should be carefully considered.

The ability we all have to develop warm, loving, and respectful relationships should be valued and nurtured in everyone. It is important to remember that the loving support of family and friends is critical to a young person coming to terms with his or her sexuality, no matter what his or her orientation.

CHAPTER 8

Talking About Values

Today's supposedly "liberated" teenagers are likely to find sex more of a worry than a joy. The boy who mentioned on TV that fear is the overriding emotion related to sex among his peers was probably not exaggerating. Suddenly, teenagers are under pressure to decide what place this new phenomenon has in their lives, how they feel about it and, most unnerving, what they personally are going to do about it. They learn quickly that it involves more confusion than glamour as they try to answer bewildering new questions of what is right and normal and embark on new kinds of relationships that bring with them new types of problems.

In addition to the factual information we have provided in this section, young people want to know a great deal more— about the intangible aspects of human sexuality. They have questions about values and impulses and pressures that they feel are too personal to ask of a school nurse or sex education teacher. They say they wish they could get the answers from their parents more often than they do. Of course, this doesn't guarantee they will always accept parental views, but that seems a risk worth taking. Sometimes they surprise you!

Among the biggest impediments to parent-teenage dialogue

about sexual matters are the adult assumptions that sex is the major concern of every adolescent and that it is focused exclusively on intercourse. This is not true of most teenagers and they resent this narrow interpretation. This sort of misunderstanding can be avoided by laying the foundation for straight talk early.

"My folks think sex is the only thing I have on my mind, which is not true at all," a sixteen-year-old girl said in a Planned Parenthood rap session. "They think if I ask about anything, it's because I'm doing it."

The fact is that most adolescents spend a lot more time thinking—and worrying—about how they look, how they should behave, romantic love, and how to make and keep friends than they do about actually having sexual intercourse themselves. There has been, understandably, so much concern about "teenage sexuality" and "teenage pregnancy" that we tend to forget most teens only know about these things second-hand.

In one survey of 625 boys and girls aged fifteen to eighteen, the girls and older boys rated "having sex" sixth out of six on a list of activities, while the fifteen- to sixteen-year-old boys rated it fifth. In all groups, having friends, doing well in school, and athletics were considered more important.

When these young people were asked how open they could be with their parents about sexual matters, 65 percent said they could not talk to them, period. Many of them mentioned that if they broached sexual questions, their parents responded by stalling—"I'm too busy to talk about it now"—teasing, or becoming angry. These aren't surprising reactions to such an emotionally weighted subject, but if parents want to encourage their teenagers to talk about what is going on in their lives, these are some things that might encourage conversation:

· Take their problems seriously. Judged by adult standards, the teenager's problem may seem trivial, but their emotions

are certainly as intense, and, to them, their difficulties seem
as real.

- Don't tease and don't let other family members—notably
brothers and sisters—indulge in it either. Teasing is basically
unkind, not funny, and it can make a hypersensitive adolescent unbelievably miserable—and hostile.

- Teenagers want their parents to trust them. They will believe
you do if you don't grill them at every opportunity but, instead, let them know that you're more interested in the qual-
ity of their lives than you are in the details.

- They want to trust parents. That means they want to know
you won't turn on them in anger if they confide in you, or that
in a jam you will stand behind them and not betray their
confidence. A wise man named John Gagnon has said, "On
the whole, no matter what bad things happen to kids, they
will be less bad if parents and kids talk to one another."

Teenage boys and girls have literally hundreds of questions
they would like to discuss with their parents about what is
happening in their lives. We have chosen a dozen of those
asked most often to respond to here.

Are Sexual Thoughts and Feelings Normal?

It is not only normal for teenagers to think about sex and feel
sexual urges, it is almost inevitable and usually nothing to
worry about. "Sometimes I can't get my mind off it. Am I going
crazy?" is a typically exaggerated adolescent worry. The sexual fantasies of boys and girls usually follow obvious gender
patterns. Those of girls are more likely to involve romance, and
dashing strangers who sweep them off their feet. Boys' fantasies tend to be more explicit, and possibly more guilt-provoking. Some boys may worry unnecessarily because they have
sexual fantasies that involve female family members. They
should be reassured that this is common, that it doesn't mean
they really want to attempt sex with a sister or with their moth-

ers. Experts agree that sexual fantasies are generally harmless and no one should feel guilty about them. In fact, the needless guilt feelings they produce are probably the most damaging thing about them. In the case of teens, sexual fantasies often substitute for a real sexual experience they're not yet ready for.

What Makes a Real Relationship? Is It Sex?

A relationship, according to the dictionary, is simply a connection between people or things, like the relationship between mother and child, student and teacher, church and state. In adolescence, a relationship between a boy and girl usually represents one further step in reaching adulthood. The potential addition of sex to such a friendship can add tension to the situation.

The idea, held by many teenagers, that a relationship isn't authentic unless it involves sex is based partly on stereotyping of male-female relationships. Adding sex into a relationship is bound to change it. Occasionally it might make the friendship stronger. More often it merely complicates a friendship and may even hasten its end.

Most teenagers, quite naturally, are not yet ready for such a commitment. It is great when boys and girls can develop happy, friendly, mutually supportive, even affectionate relationships with one another. If they have a good relationship, they should think about what aspects of it are important to them. They shouldn't let themselves feel pressured to progress to something more "meaningful."

When Are You Old Enough to Have Sex?

A great many teenagers would love to know—but dare not ask—their parents how old *they* were when they started having sexual relations. They wonder how *they* felt about it and dealt with it. This isn't purely curiosity. The would-be questioners are struggling with an enormous decision and would like to use the most obvious role models, their parents, for help in making it.

Parents don't need to discuss their private lives, if they don't care to, in order to be helpful to their children. On the other hand, they're wasting breath if they simply command their teens to postpone sexual activity because it is wrong at their age, or dangerous, or against parental principles. None of the above tells teenagers anything they need to know.

Instead, parents should take the opportunity to help their sons and daughters sort out their feelings, and make a more intelligent choice, by suggesting that they ask themselves why they're considering sexual involvement. Is it because of their own strong urges, or because of social pressure? Is it because society has given them the idea that virginity is a "burden" to be gotten rid of? Do they think it will make them more popular or help them keep a boyfriend or girlfriend? Is it to punish parents or get more attention from them? If the answer is "yes" to any of these questions, the teenager needs help putting things into perspective.

Most adolescents simply have not yet achieved the emotional and intellectual maturity required to handle a sexual relationship noninjuriously for themselves or their partners. To be truly ready for sex, persons must:

- be sure they are not exploiting another person or being exploited themselves.
- be able to discuss comfortably with their partner precautions against unintended pregnancy and STDs and to share responsibility for taking them.
- be able to accept the consequences of their own actions. Could they deal with a pregnancy or with contracting a disease?
- be willing to make the emotional commitment and take on the obligations of a healthy adult sexual relationship.
- understand that enjoying this aspect of sexuality involves

the ability to make thoughtful decisions. Without this, the sex act is likely to produce far more stress and anxiety than pleasure.

Are You Supposed to Enjoy Sex the First Time?

Whether they're supposed to or not, the fact is that even many adults don't for a number of reasons. It takes experience, patience, understanding, and caring to give and receive sexual satisfaction. It is not an ability people are automatically born with. Teenagers especially are likely to find their first sexual experiences disappointing. They probably lack the necessary information about how each other's bodies work; they may be so afraid of being caught that they are hurried and fumbling; guilt about doing something that may be in conflict with parents' values, and worry about performance don't leave much room for caring about the other person. A girl who has an intact hymen (the thin piece of skin just inside the vagina) may find penetration painful and have some bleeding. Unless her first experience is with a knowledgeable and patient partner, the odds are against a girl reaching orgasm the first time she has sex.

Do Boys and Girls Have Different Views About Sex?

They most certainly do, and their common failure to understand where the other person is coming from leads to a lot of confusion and, frequently, to unhappy, short-lived relationships. Girls traditionally have been raised in our society to believe that love and romance must be tied in with sex, while often boys have been conditioned to believe that "scoring" is what counts. As a result, what girls really want more than sexual intercourse is closeness, intimacy, tenderness, caring—all qualities boys have been *taught* they should spurn although they too may want these qualities in a relationship.

Girls are thought of as giving sex, boys as taking it. Being reared with this belief can cause misunderstanding and anger between the sexes if boys see girls as "flaunting it" but not giving it, and girls see boys as having all the power in the relationship. This is changing in our society, but very slowly.

The risks in a sexual relationship are also different for boys and for girls and quite unevenly weighted. The centuries-old belief that pregnancy is solely a woman's responsibility is slow to die. However, it is still the case that only girls can get pregnant.

In sum, boys and girls have been reared to want and expect different things from their interaction with one another. At the age when they begin to be attracted to and form relationships with one another, they still haven't developed much understanding of the other sex or much skill in communicating. This is probably the best argument of all for taking teenage relationships slowly.

How Do You Say "No" Without Hurting the Other Person's Feelings?

A survey of sexually active girls under sixteen revealed that the information they wanted most was how to refuse a boy's advances diplomatically. These teenagers didn't necessarily want to have sexual relations and did so because they lacked the social skills to deal with the situation.

The scenario is a familiar one, unfortunately, for many young teenage girls. For the first time in her life a boy is paying attention to her. Moreover, it is a boy she has been secretly admiring. Typically, he is a year or two older than she, which gives him an added psychological advantage. His interest makes her feel that she is beautiful, life is meaningful, all is bliss. Soon the boy is pressuring her to become more sexually involved than she wants to be. She doesn't know of any way to turn him down without losing him, so she gives in.

To say "no" gracefully is especially hard for teenagers who

haven't yet developed much social prowess and whose perspective is quite limited. Girls and boys really need to be prepared by their parents for the possibility of this situation and supported if they encounter it. Declining a sexual relationship should not mean the end of the friendship, if the boy and girl value one another and the other activities they share.

If there is open communication, parents can anticipate these situations and discuss them. As with questions about the physical aspects of sex, we recommend talking about the dynamics of teenage relationships with youngsters before they reach that age. Explain the pressures, both societal and hormonal, they will feel and the pressures they will feel compelled to put on others. Make sure they understand that a relationship that is not mutual is not really worth having. Remember that these conflicts are not exclusive to adolescents, either. Adults struggle with decisions regarding the way their relationships are to be organized too. For everyone there should be an equal sharing of motives, concern, and respect. It is important for young people to consider the outcomes of their decisions in light of their plans for the future. Remind them that they will be attracted to many members of the opposite sex and vice versa before they reach maturity. If your message is given at that time, it is more likely to sink in.

Parents can be extremely supportive without being obtrusive if their child is seeking to delay an involvement he or she doesn't feel ready for. They wouldn't admit it for the world, but many young teens are secretly grateful to their parents for setting curfews and dating rules and standards of behavior that give them a graceful way out of a tight spot.

How Can You Put Off Having Sex When Everyone Else Is Doing It?

It's hard for adults to remember the power of peer pressure among teens. It is enormous. Just ask anyone in business who deals with that market. "When one of the young ladies has to

have something, they all do. It's like mass hysteria." This is the
way a fashion designer recently described it to the *Wall Street
Journal.*

These business people who depend on the teen market have
learned, perhaps to their sorrow, that teenagers have a fragile
sense of self. They are still trying to figure out who they are,
and consequently their personal beliefs are not well enough
established for them to feel comfortable making independent
choices.

Another fact that adults may have forgotten is that pressure
to enter into sexual activity is by no means directed exclusively at young girls by young boys with very active sex drives.
There is possibly more pressure put on boys than on girls. The
pressure is basically societal and originates among peers of
their own gender.

Adolescents want desperately to be liked, admired, and
looked up to, not down on. Above all, they want to be accepted
by their contemporaries. When the message comes from every
side, and it does, that to be accepted one must be sexually
active, teenagers can feel very threatened. It can help to stiffen
their children's resolve to act on their own feelings if parents
reassure them that what they do with their bodies is their business and no one else's, that anyone who tries to force them into
having sex is, knowingly or not, trying to exploit them. Teenagers need to hear that they have the freedom to make their
own choices and that they are not abnormal if they want to put
off sex.

Which Partner Is Supposed to Be Responsible for Birth Control?

Both partners are. Avoiding pregnancy has traditionally been
considered a female responsibility, like keeping house or raising children. Those times are beginning to change, although the
message hasn't filtered down to the teenage world yet. Stereotyping of roles and responsibilities by gender is giving way to a

sharing by men and women of tasks and duties, professions and pleasures. Today, there is a trend toward making relationships real partnerships.

Being able to talk to a sexual partner about birth control and sharing responsibility for using it are marks of a mature relationship. Most teenagers would agree that it is important to take responsibility for preventing an unwanted pregnancy, but once again, there is a perceptible gap between their beliefs and their behavior.

By sixteen or so, boys may develop a stronger sense of responsibility, but their self-confidence may not be sufficiently developed to allow them to attempt using a condom for fear they will bungle it and look inexperienced. Appearing macho may be more important than being responsible. Sex educators believe it is imperative for parents to talk about the need for shared responsibility concerning birth control with boys and to get them to think about what sex means to them. If the gap between adolescent beliefs and adolescent behavior could be narrowed in just this area, the number of unintended pregnancies in the United States would drop perceptibly.

Is Oral Sex a Perversion? Will It Hurt Me?

This is a question most teenagers would feel too uncomfortable to ask anyone, but it ranks near the top of lists of questions they ask anonymously. The subject may be taboo to talk about, but the practice is becoming increasingly widespread among adolescents as a way to avoid pregnancy. As a result, many young people worry that enjoying it means they are abnormal. Most sex educators would tell them that oral sex is a form of sexual expression which many people find pleasurable and many others find unthinkable. Sexual behavior that is mutually agreed on and harmful to neither partner is not considered a perversion. Young people should be aware, though, that several STDs can be transmitted through oral sex as well as through intercourse. (See earlier discussion of STDs.)

Is It Abnormal to Want to Wait Till I'm Older to Have Sex?

No, it is not, despite all the pressures to the contrary. Many young people feel they want to wait for a variety of reasons. They may realize they aren't ready to handle the psychological effects of a sexual relationship or that early sex would make them feel guilty or anxious. Some may be afraid of becoming too emotionally dependent on a partner. Some may want to wait until after marriage. Others may have interests that keep them too busy to think much about sex. Some people are "late bloomers," or may never develop a very strong sex drive. Even though the media most often portray sex as just another form of recreation, many young people still feel they want it to represent something more important in their lives. Deciding for oneself the when and why and how of personal sexual behavior is one of the most confusing and complex processes human beings must go through, but a teenager who has gotten as far as understanding that there are such decisions to be made is well on the way to maturity.

What's Wrong with Sex for Teens If They're Responsible?

Responsible presumably means avoiding pregnancy and disease, the two most obviously disastrous results of teenage sexual activity. However, responsibility for one's own actions and life goes far beyond this, and most people believe that, responsible or not, intercourse is an experience that should be postponed until adulthood and marriage. Parents particularly feel that way, not necessarily for moral reasons but because they want the best for their children in every way. Many young boys and girls are not emotionally experienced enough to deal with the strong emotions a sexual relationship can create. Once a person becomes sexually active, he or she may have more than one partner during adolescence; the repeated breaking up of relationships that include a sexual involvement can be emotionally devastating. If they know their parents would be deeply opposed, many kids can't handle the guilt feelings that accompany their sexual activity. Young adolescents, at least in present-day Western society, have so many other growing-up tasks to accomplish that sexual intercourse is best postponed till later in their lives.

How Do You Know When You're in Love?

"Falling in love" is probably the most thrilling experience people enjoy. It can happen over and over again, often at a moment's notice. It produces emotional highs and lows like nothing else can. It often possesses teenagers entirely, leaving them little time or energy or interest for anything but savoring or suffering this ecstatic new sensation. A more accurate name for it is infatuation.

Its most interesting aspect to onlookers, though, is how little infatuation has to do with reality. A girl notices the curly hair on the nape of a boy's neck and—presto!—she's "in love" with him. A boy watches the way a girl moves or smiles or tells a joke and suddenly he's in love. The real person, the possessor of a character, interests, tastes, feelings—qualities that can inspire real, mature love—is totally unknown and unimportant to the teenager in love. The whole encounter is a fantasy, as kids who ask, "How do you know when you're in love?" must suspect.

This doesn't mean that parents should disparage or discourage teenage romances. These experiences are a necessary part of maturation. And they are an important way of learning to interact with other people on a new level.

The concern lies in teenagers' mistaken belief, fostered by their music, their reading, their favorite TV shows, their favorite showbiz personalities and the lack of communication with parents, that this feeling is the real thing and that it is a justification for their having sexual intercourse. They need to understand the distinction between love and infatuation and know that real love isn't used as a weapon. "If you loved me you would" is a line every girl, and some boys, have heard and too many have succumbed to. Sex should never be used as a test of love, and sexual intimacy doesn't equal love, no matter what the lyrics say.

Beyond the excitement of sexual feelings, love involves respect for who the other person is and for what they do with their lives. Sharing in a broad range of activities with their peers is a good way for young people to learn about the ways in which their relationship may be loving or special.

PART III

Help in Special Situations

CHAPTER 9

Facing Facts

Unless they are confronted with undeniable evidence, many parents won't face the possibility that their teenager is involved in a sexual relationship. The discovery of such a situation may be deeply disturbing for several reasons. Since parents usually have made it clear they would disapprove, it means their advice has not been taken. Such intimacy with someone else also makes them aware that their child could soon reach adulthood. Perhaps most painful of all is the fear that their son or daughter will be compromised or hurt by the relationship. These feelings all make it hard for many parents to acknowledge or discuss their child's sexual activity. The end result can be a "conspiracy of silence" because adolescents are equally reluctant to talk about something that they know, or fear, will upset or make their parents angry. This reluctance, added to their own feelings of personal privacy about their sexual behavior, often adds up to a stalemate.

If parents want to truly protect their sons and daughters from potential tragedy, parents, uncomfortable as it may be for them, must go beyond saying they would be very angry or disappointed to learn of any premature sexual activity. And, whether their children admit it or not, they really want their parents to say more. Of 160,000 teens questioned for a survey, nearly all wanted more information from parents on birth control and venereal diseases (or, as they are referred to now, sexually transmissible diseases). Although almost one third of the thirteen- to fifteen-year-olds in this survey were already having intercourse, 71 percent of the entire group said that they had never discussed contraception with their parents.

Even if parents believe their views on early sexual activity will be rejected by their teens, they should let their children know them, clearly, honestly, and calmly. A 1985 survey commissioned by Planned Parenthood asked over twelve hundred U.S. adults whether they feel that parents have any control over their teenager's sexual activity. Only about one third of the respondents feel that parents have any such control. What then, we asked, are parents to do? In response to this open-ended question, 35 percent of the respondents said that the most important thing parents can do is talk with their children about sex and sexuality, another 17 percent felt that parents should explain contraceptive methods, and another 13 percent felt that the most important thing parents can do is to explain the risks and consequences of pregnancy.

"I" messages are important in communication. In other words, it may be most helpful for a parent to convey this message by saying something like, "I am truly concerned that you have the information you need so that when you decide to have intercourse you can protect yourself from an unintended pregnancy." We say again, this message needs to be relayed to sons as well as to daughters. If the teenager's response is, as it might well be, "Oh, Mother, I know all that stuff, they talked about it in school," or, more simply, "Oh, Mother!" we encourage you to persevere. If need be, ask for their indulgence, "Well, maybe you think you know, but I, for me, need to tell you one more time, so bear with me." You are a parent, and, as such, what you say now is backed with all the concern and love you have given your child over a lifetime. This may carry considerably more clout than other message-deliverers.

Discussing contraception—which is vitally important, we stress again—does not mean and is seldom interpreted by teenagers to mean that you have given permission for them to have intercourse. No study has *ever* shown that the children of parents who have discussed sex, sexuality, and contraception with them are more likely to have intercourse than the children of parents who believe that ignorance is bliss. But one study showed that girls whose mothers have talked with them about birth control are *more* likely to use an effective means of contraception when they do have sex, than are girls who say their mothers have not talked with them about such matters.

By the same token, we hope parents will be more relieved than angry if they find their children have acquired contraceptives. It is true that these young people may seem to be rejecting their parents' values, at one level, by having intercourse. However, at a deeper level, they are expressing other important values—the need to be responsible for avoiding unintended and unwanted pregnancy.

At Planned Parenthood we encourage teenagers to ask their parents to help them with their contraceptive decisions. We recognize that young people know their particular parents better than we do, however, and that teens are better judges of whether such discussions are possible.

"I don't believe Sally and Jim should be having sex," a mother said to us recently. "I told her so and why. After all, she is only fifteen. Sally has always been a girl who does what she wants and I could see she wasn't hearing my concerns. So I was quite surprised when I asked that she and Jim at least go to Planned Parenthood for counseling and birth control if they were going to have sex and they agreed. I really think they were grateful."

"When I found Crissy's birth control pills I was furious," a California mother confided in us. "Luckily she was at school, and I had time to think about my reaction before I spoke to her. Though it upsets me to know she's having sex, I know that my messages about responsible sex have gotten through."

AND DEALING WITH CONSEQUENCES

Every year, hundreds of thousands of young girls have their worst fears confirmed at family planning clinics and doctors' offices around the country. They are pregnant. Almost invariably, the first frightened reaction is: "How am I going to tell my parents?"

In many cases, they can go to their parents for help and guidance. In other cases, however, they cannot—or feel they cannot—and so they may deny the pregnancy, run away from home, go through an abortion secretly, or even commit suicide —all tragic choices. At Planned Parenthood, we encourage girls who are pregnant to give their parents the opportunity to help them, hard as it may be to break the news, and painful as it may be for parents to receive it. A counselor with many years of experience says, "I tell them they can expect their parents will be very upset and angry, but that once they work through the anger they will want to help them."

It is certainly natural for parents to feel a range of overwhelming emotions upon learning, or suspecting, that a young child of theirs is pregnant. Anger, feelings of failure as a parent, betrayal and, finally, pain at the problems in store for the child are typical reactions. But there can be room for more positive feelings, too. The parents of a pregnant fifteen-year-old put it this way: "Once we got over the initial shock and outrage we realized it was a pretty good sign that Suky felt she could come to us with her problem. It meant she believed our relationship was strong enough to stand it."

Even a relationship which has been less than perfect in the past can be strengthened when parents decide to see a daughter or son through a crisis of this kind.

It is not at all uncommon for a frightened teenager to deal with a pregnancy by denying it. Therefore, parents who have any reason to suspect a daughter might be pregnant should not wait for her to tell them but should ask her. If you suspect that your daughter is pregnant and she responds to your asking by denying it, it's important to make clear to her that she has options and alternatives. Tell her you're concerned about her and that you recognize that she may feel unable to talk with you about this. As with any discussion of sexual activity with your teenager, suggest the availability of services and counseling from health care agencies and professionals. You may feel comfortable suggesting that she talk to another adult whom both of you trust: a friend, relative, teacher, or church person. If there seems to be any possibility of pregnancy, try to make sure she has a test right away. There are two extremely important reasons to confirm a pregnancy as early as possible. One is that the earlier a pregnancy is recognized, the greater the number of choices to consider. The other is that the health of both mother and baby, if the pregnancy is continued, are crucially affected by care and nutrition in the early months.

A pregnancy test can be done after a woman has missed one period. It will show whether a certain hormone related to pregnancy is present in her body. A urine or a blood test can show the pregnancy hormone within days after the missed period. There are do-it-yourself pregnancy tests that can be bought in a drugstore, but they may not be as accurate as early as a laboratory test and may be difficult to read. They can give both false negative and false positive results. Furthermore the diagnosis of pregnancy, and particularly its duration, must be established by performance of a physical assessment that includes a pelvic examination. So it is wiser and perhaps more reliable to have the test done by a physician, family planning clinic, or a laboratory.

As soon as pregnancy is confirmed, the girl needs to begin considering the various possibilities. If she can talk this over with her parents—fine! If she feels she cannot, or if the family needs help to work through their feelings until they can consider the situation objectively, either the girl or the family can ask Planned Parenthood, their minister or rabbi, or a community mental health center to refer them to a counselor.

The "Decision Tree" depicts in graph form the considerations each alternative involves. This Decision Tree traces out the steps a woman can take when she is faced with an unintended pregnancy. Her first decision is whether to carry the pregnancy to term or to choose abortion. The sooner that decision is made, the better.

To illustrate the next steps, look at the "branch" of the tree marked "full-term pregnancy." A health care professional should be consulted as soon as possible to advise on the proper care of the expectant mother and the baby. One of the most important decisions to be made is whether to keep the baby or place it for adoption. There are several agencies in every state that coordinate adoption; later in the chapter we discuss where to find them. If the young woman chooses adoption, she may opt to live at home with her family or stay in a maternity home where she can share in the support of other girls who have made a similar decision. For those who decide not to place the child for adoption, the question may arise whether the pregnant teenager and the baby's father will marry. The feasibility of this decision is a complex issue that is discussed in this chapter, as is the decision to raise the child without marriage. As is noted later, establishing paternity is an important step in this branch of the decision-making process and involves economic as well as emotional considerations. Whichever options are chosen, a postpartum checkup and contraceptive plan are needed to ensure the health and well-being of the young woman.

On the other side of the decision-making tree is "termination." Abortions can be done in clinics or by private physicians. Private physicians do abortions in their offices or, especially for abortions performed later in the pregnancy, in hospitals. Abortions performed later in the pregnancy are more likely to be performed in hospitals. No matter where the abortion is performed, the woman should have a post-abortion checkup and also make a contraceptive plan to avoid further unintended pregnancies.

DECISION TREE FOR WOMEN FACED WITH AN UNINTENDED PREGNANCY

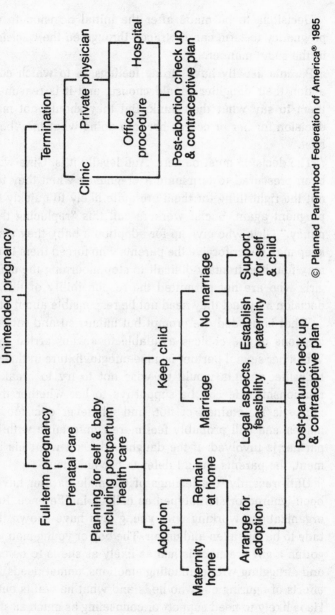

Unintended pregnancy

Termination
- Clinic
- Private physician
  - Office procedure
  - Hospital
- Post-abortion check up & contraceptive plan

Full-term pregnancy
- Prenatal care
- Planning for self & baby including postpartum health care

Adoption
- Maternity home
- Remain at home
  - Arrange for adoption

Keep child
- Marriage
  - Legal aspects, feasibility
- No marriage
  - Establish paternity
  - Support for self & child
- Post-partum check up & contraceptive plan

© Planned Parenthood Federation of America® 1985

Decisions to be made after the initial decision to carry a pregnancy to term can be traced through on the Decision Tree in the same manner.

Parents usually have strong feelings as to which course of action their daughter should choose, and it is reasonable for them to say what they think. But they should not make the decision for her or coerce her into doing what *they* believe is best.

The decision must be hers. And legally it is. Girls who have been pressured to terminate a pregnancy when they feel it is not the right thing for them are quite likely to quickly become pregnant again. Social workers call this "replacing the pregnancy." Girls who give up for adoption a baby they wanted to keep may never forgive the parents who forced them to do it, or may find it extremely difficult to stop mourning the child. And girls who are not permitted the responsibility of this critical decision may feel they need not be responsible about anything.

What is needed are prompt but unhurried and rational discussions of the choices available to an unmarried teenager. When her sexual partner is a meaningful fixture in their daughter's life, parents would be wise not to try to break up the relationship. He can be supportive to her whether the pregnancy is maintained or not, and whatever decision the girl makes, she will probably feel more comfortable with it if her partner is involved. If the daughter doesn't want his involvement, the parents should defer to her judgment.

Until recently, the feelings of the male partner have either been ignored or stereotyped as callous indifference. Recently, organizations working with young men have shown this attitude to be mistaken and unfair. The boy or young man who has gotten a girl pregnant is just as likely as she is to be confused and struggling with conflicting emotions, unmet needs, and the efforts of figuring out who he is and what he wants out of life. He is likely to need support or counseling as much as she does. Many boys say they would like to maintain their relationship with the girl and with their baby, if she keeps it, but that her parents shut them out.

Whatever becomes of the relationship between the young couple, it is more important than most people realize to establish paternity whenever the mother chooses to maintain the pregnancy and keep the child. The most obvious reasons are economic. A father is required by law to support his child, no matter how young he is. Establishing paternity also gives the child future access to Social Security benefits, disability and veterans' benefits, pensions, and other rights of inheritance. The stigma of out-of-wedlock birth is still with us, but it is a little less painful for children who at least know who their father is. Research has shown that children who don't know their parentage often find it difficult to develop a strong sense of identity. And the father-child relationship is one both of them have a right to. Finally, there are sound medical reasons to establish paternity, for the possibility exists of passing on to the next generation genetic diseases or defects inherited from the father.

Sometimes a boy denies that he is the father of his girlfriend's child. The truth can be determined with 95 percent accuracy by a blood test. According to a pamphlet recently published by the U.S. Department of Health and Human Services, "a very large percentage of paternity cases can now be resolved out of court at reasonable cost and with great reliability." Resolution of paternity must be done before a petition can be filed for child support and, in some states, before an unmarried mother can receive AFDC (Aid to Families with Dependent Children) benefits.

One of the sad truths a pregnant teenager must face is that none of the choices available to her is very attractive. Another possibility is to marry the father of her child. If she and the boy are considering this, they should be counseled that teenage marriages have an especially poor success rate. Over half of them end in separation or divorce within a few years. Rather than solve the problem of the pregnancy, premature marriage is more likely to put the futures of three human beings in jeopardy. In fact, fewer young women are marrying "to legitimate the pregnancy" than was the case twenty years ago. The proportion of young women ages twenty to twenty-four who have not yet married is growing every year, as young women postpone marriage into their late twenties. The proportion of young women under twenty who are married is also declining. Long-term studies of the education and earnings of women who marry young and have children while still teenagers show that they are less likely to go on with their education, and, while more likely to work, less likely to have high earnings. In sum, teenage marriages, with or without an attendant pregnancy and birth, are likely to be disastrous for the overwhelming majority of young women who enter into them.

Here we would put in a note about research. No doubt many people can recite an "exception to the rule." We have to remember that most research is based on large numbers of individuals and what is "most likely" to be the case. Not everyone who marries young or who has a child out of wedlock will suffer these negative outcomes. The risk, however, is very great, and that's what we are talking about.

Some girls decide to have the baby and give it up for adoption. Recently, there have been more white families wanting to adopt children, and fewer white children to adopt. So many young women can be almost certain that there is a family that really wants to adopt the child. Sadly this is not always true for Black and Latino children. The decision to place a child for adoption is often a difficult one to make. A girl considering placing her child for adoption should realize that conflicting emotions are very common. Very often feelings of sadness and ambivalence are combined with feelings of relief and the conviction that her decision was the right one for her. Adoption professionals are available to help in making the best possible decision for the birth parents and the child.

Although the birth parents do not make a final decision about adoption until after the baby is born, contacting a licensed adoption agency early in the pregnancy will allow everyone more time to examine what is best for the birth parents and the child. Your local Planned Parenthood, health or social service agency can help in locating such an adoption agency. The agency will have experienced professionals whose job it is to help the birth parents in examining all of the options they have.

The father's role in the adoption process is an important issue for birth parents to discuss with a counselor. In some states, the father of a child has the legal right to present his views concerning the adoption. An unmarried father may have the same legal rights as a married father, if paternity has been established. If the father is opposed to placing the child for adoption, in some states he must present an alternative plan for raising the child. If this plan is approved by the court, the child cannot be placed for adoption.

In some states, birth parents eighteen years or older are not required by law to involve their parents in the adoption decision. However, birth parents often choose to involve family members because of the support and guidance they can offer. If the birth parents are under eighteen, a parent or guardian may have to be present at the adoption proceedings.

If a young woman does decide on adoption, it is usually recommended that she give up the baby at birth. Many birth parents request certain qualities that they consider important in an adoptive family. These qualities are taken into consideration when a home for the child is being selected. The adoption agency screens adoptive parents carefully and considers many factors when selecting an adoptive family. These factors include marital stability, child-raising philosophy, age, health, religion, income, and race. Non-identifying information about the adoptive parents may be shared with the birth parents at their request. Also, if they need to, both the birth mother and the child may have a better chance of finding each other years later if the adoption took place through a recognized agency where formal records were kept of the adoption.

Today, a growing number of teenage girls are keeping their babies. Many professionals believe this trend of teenage parenting is as great a concern as teenage pregnancy. Adolescent girls are still busy with the tasks of growing up, and combining these with motherhood places a heavy burden on both the mother and the baby. Studies have shown that the success or failure of teenage parenting depends a great deal on the amount of support of all kinds the girl receives from her family.

One unfortunate consequence of a teenager's going through with the pregnancy and keeping the baby is that she is likely to drop out of school and never go back. Statistics show that only a very small percentage of unmarried teenage mothers finish school, which gives them a severe handicap in earning a living. Pregnant teenagers need to be encouraged to stay in school, and the law states that any school receiving federal aid may not discriminate against them. More and more public schools are developing programs for pregnant girls and many communities now offer special parenting courses for young mothers and fathers. Family planning clinics and social service agencies are aware of where these courses are and what they offer.

Even more serious than neglect of her education is the average teenager's neglect of her health during the pregnancy. Medical studies show that the biological risks associated with teenage childbearing (except for very young mothers) are mainly due to poor prenatal care. So it is just as vital to have early confirmation of a pregnancy that will be maintained as it is of one that will be terminated. Drinking, smoking, and abusing drugs are all injurious to the fetus, and there are also certain medically prescribed drugs (for seizures and for acne, among others) that can be dangerous to the fetus and should be avoided. If she wants to give her baby a good start, a teenage mother is likely to have to radically change her eating habits. She will need solid information, plenty of encouragement, and extra willpower to stick to a sensible diet. Your local Planned Parenthood center can refer you for prenatal care.

Young girls commonly harbor a variety of unrealistic ideas

about motherhood. When an adolescent says she wants to keep her baby, it may be for any of the following reasons:

- She thinks it will give her adult status.
- She feels unloved and believes a baby will provide love.
- She wants to escape from her family.
- She hopes to stabilize the relationship with her boyfriend.
- She is trying to change the relationship with her parents.
- She may be morally opposed to abortion.
- She is so guilty about having had a sexual relationship that she feels she should go through with the pregnancy as a punishment, or to take "responsibility" for the consequences of her behavior.

Parents may be able to help a daughter be realistic about her reasons for continuing a pregnancy. Although you are a parent and not a counselor, some tips from those who counsel adolescents might be of assistance. One way to help your daughter look at her reasons for wanting to keep her baby is to explore which of her own needs that reason fills. Another way is to ask what she expects her life will be like with the baby and without it. This helps her look at fantasies in the "cool light of day." It could be very helpful to contact a local school-age pregnancy program and ask if your daughter can talk to a young mother who has chosen to have and keep her child. Again, it will help for you to remember that the decision must be hers. You owe her the facts about what you can or will do to help. At least make sure she has an opportunity to talk with a family counselor who can help her see the situation more clearly without the emotional loading. If some other way of satisfying her needs can be suggested, she can make a sounder choice about the future.

The fourth course open to the pregnant teenager is to end the pregnancy. If she—together with her parents, we hope—has considered all the choices and decided that this is the most appropriate one for her, federal law guarantees her the right to an abortion performed by a licensed physician. In some states, the law requires that the parents of a minor be notified, or that they give consent. In those states, she has the choice of obtaining parental consent or having consent granted in court. She is entitled to a confidential hearing where she must have an opportunity to demonstrate that she is mature enough to make a decision about abortion. In other states there is no parental consent or notice required.

Abortion done in the first three months of pregnancy (up to the fourteenth week since the onset of the last period) is simplest and safest. At this time the procedure can be done in a doctor's office or a clinic and the patient goes home after a brief recovery period. Abortion in the middle three months of pregnancy is more complex and may involve an overnight stay in or near a clinic or hospital, especially toward the sixth month of the pregnancy. Ending a pregnancy in the last three months is done only when there are serious medical reasons, and hospitalization is required.

The most common method of abortion in the first fourteen weeks (first trimester) of pregnancy is called "vacuum aspiration." The procedure, which is done with a local anesthetic, usually takes less than ten minutes and may cause some menstrual-like cramps. There should be someone waiting to accompany the patient home.

Beginning with the fourth month of pregnancy, a combination method called "dilation and evacuation" (D&E) is most commonly used. When it is done in a clinic, it usually requires two successive visits by the patient. There is a much greater chance of such complications as bleeding, infection, incomplete abortion, and perforation of the uterus than with an earlier abortion, but at no time do they exceed the risks of pregnancy carried to term. Recovery time at the clinic after the procedure is usually an hour or two.

After about the fifth month, hospitalization is required and techniques are used that cause contractions and expulsion of the fetus. This usually calls for an overnight stay or longer. The risks of complications are greater than for D&E.

Because the prospect of an abortion can be frightening, it may tempt a pregnant teenager to put off the procedure. We emphasize again that the earlier an abortion is done the safer it is. Risks increase greatly in the later weeks. As in any kind of surgery, it is possible for problems to develop, but in the great majority of cases they are minor, including nothing more than cramping, upset stomach or moderate bleeding for a short time. The risks associated with abortion are considerably less than those associated with continuing a pregnancy. Published data also indicate that the risks associated with FDA-approved contraceptives for young women are much lower than the risks associated with pregnancy.

An early abortion is also far less expensive than a late one. Costs range from about $200 for one done early, in a clinic, to over $1,000 for a late abortion done in a hospital. It is a good idea to ask about fees and payment method ahead of time. Some health insurance policies cover all or part of the cost— another reason for a teenager to talk it over with her parents. In all states, Medicaid will pay for an abortion for eligible recipients when the life of the mother is in danger, and in some states it will pay under other circumstances as well.

Anyone who has had an abortion should have a medical checkup two to four weeks later to make sure everything is back to normal. Most abortion services include this exam in their initial fee. It can be done by a private doctor or in a family planning clinic.

A very important fact that teenagers should clearly understand is that abortion is not a substitute for contraception. After an abortion, or a delivery, for that matter, a teenager needs to have a serious talk with either her parents or a health professional about contraception, whether she believes she is going to resume sexual activity or not. Girls are often so traumatized by the pregnancy that they vow, "I'm never going to have sex again!" She should be helped to understand that this is a common reaction and that she is very likely to change her mind. In fact, 7.9 percent of abortions to women under nineteen are repeat abortions.

CHAPTER 10

Protecting Children From Sexual Abuse

Sexual abuse can take many forms and human beings of all ages can be its victims. The molestation of young children and the rape of older ones by adults, or their peers, are particularly horrifying, but until recent years they were rarely talked about. Now a rash of highly publicized cases has turned a national spotlight on sexual abuse of young children. Although frightening, this can be a good thing because when parents are informed, they can do a great deal to make sure it doesn't happen to their children or to minimize its impact if it does.

WHAT PARENTS SHOULD KNOW ABOUT CHILD MOLESTATION

Government officials describe the sexual abuse of children as one of this country's most frequent and least understood crimes. It is estimated that as many as 25 percent of girls and over 10 percent of boys may be victims of some type of sexual abuse before they reach age thirteen. The Federal Bureau of Investigation further claims that less than 10 percent of incidents are reported. Victims are most frequently young children, typically eight years old or younger.

Probably the most common misconception about child molestation is that it is committed by a sinister stranger who lures a child into his car or basement. On that premise many parents believe that if they warn their children never to get into a stranger's car or go home with him or her they have told them all the children need to know.

Although it is true that the majority of abusers are adult heterosexual males (with boys and women accounting for a very small percentage of cases), they are rarely strangers—70 to 80 percent of offenders are known to the child. Very possibly it is a man the child trusts or even loves who commits this crime.

Incest, particularly in stepfamilies, is far more common than most people realize. It is estimated by child welfare experts that one half the cases of child sexual abuse occur within a family. The American Humane Association has figures of 48,000 *reported* cases in 1982. The dynamics of incest are far more complicated and devastating than of sexual abuse by someone unrelated. Incestuous parents can love their children but for a variety of reasons, including their own views on sexuality and frequently their own past history of being abused, put their needs ahead of the child's well-being.

The victim of incest is even less likely than other abuse victims to tell anyone what is happening because of fear of the consequences. It can mean breakup of the family, prison for the offender, or rejection of the victim by the rest of the family members. A high proportion of runaways are boys and girls who were being sexually abused at home. However, unless this serious problem is admitted and help is found, the abuse will probably continue for a number of years and may also focus on other children in the family.

Along with the picture of the sinister man in the car goes the mistaken idea that child abuse is likely to be a single, isolated incident. More often it continues for months, even for several years. The offender commonly uses a combination of threats and bribes to make sure the child tells no one of what is happening.

Sexual abuse of children can take a variety of forms. Professionals define it as any sexual contact—by force, trickery, or bribery—where there is an imbalance in age, size, power, or knowledge. It can include fondling, obscene phone calls, exhibitionism, masturbation, intercourse, oral or anal sex, prostitution, or pornography.

Sexual abusers come from every walk of life, social class, and religious background. They can range in age from twelve to ninety. They may be married or single; they are much more likely to be heterosexual than homosexual. And they usually appear perfectly normal to other adults.

Child abusers prey on boys and girls who clearly lack self-confidence or have a poor opinion of themselves. They look for children who are easily manipulated and are vulnerable to their offers of friendship and rewards. Children who are obviously self-reliant or assertive may be less attracted to such lures.

HOW TO PREVENT CHILD ABUSE

Although society has always been aware that child molestation takes place, in the past many parents were reluctant to warn children about it for fear of frightening them. The statistics now available on its prevalence make it clear that a warning is as vital a piece of survival information as teaching preschoolers not to play with matches or dash into the street. Warnings can be given in ways that are neither frightening nor confusing. Some schools have begun to include simple hour-long programs in kindergarten and the early grades that teach young children to recognize potentially threatening situations with adults. Many of the techniques they use can be adapted by parents to teach their children how to protect themselves.

Most professionals suggest that parents begin their safety teaching when children are four or five years old and are no longer as closely supervised as they have been earlier. The need to do this reinforces the importance of talking to very young children about sexuality in general. It is just as important for children not to believe that all sexual behavior is bad or hurtful as it is for them to understand when they are supposed to say no. One way to do this in a nonfrightening manner and on a level they can comprehend is to explain the difference between good touching and bad touching. A good touch is one that feels comfortable or comforting to them. A bad touch is any contact that makes them uncomfortable or actually hurts them physically. Children should be told that if any adult touches them in that way, they should tell a parent or other trusted adult right away, and they should be assured that they will be believed.

If parents insist their children give and receive all sorts of displays of physical affection from relatives and adult family friends, it makes it difficult for the youngsters to sort out whom they can say no to. It's best to let *them* decide whether they want to let Grandpa or Uncle Bob give them a hug or kiss.

It isn't a good idea to tell youngsters that only mean, bad, sick, or crazy people do things like this. Very often molesters do not fit any of those categories in the child's eyes. In fact, the majority first befriend their victims, or are family friends. It is usually sufficient to say that there are some people who *seem* okay but who like to do things they shouldn't do with children. For this reason, youngsters should know that while they are usually supposed to do what adults tell them for their own good, they do not *always* have to obey *every* adult, even family members. If someone offers them presents for doing something or tells them it must be kept a secret, they should refuse. Secrets are all right only if, like a surprise for someone, they can be shared at some point.

"What if . . . ," a game that is useful for teaching children about safety in general, is a good way to describe potentially dangerous situations or people and to explain how children should respond. "What if you got separated from me in a crowd?" a parent asks. "Would you know what to do?" or "What if I didn't come to get you at school one day?" In the same way, questions like "What if a strange man offered you a ride home from the playground?" or "What if the baby-sitter said you could stay up later if you let him put his hand in your pants?" can be used to teach children how *not* to respond to sexually threatening situations.

Earlier in this book we recommended teaching young children the correct names for anatomical parts. The importance of doing this is frequently seen when attempts are made to prosecute sexual offenders. In a widely publicized case in 1984, a young child told investigators she had been "hurt where I go poop." The defendants insisted she was referring either to a spanking or a time when she had to be frequently wiped because of diarrhea. It is often difficult to get a coherent account of what took place if the child doesn't know the correct terminology.

Boys are not often asked to baby-sit. This may be because it is seen as "women's work" and not masculine; however, parents may also have an unspoken fear that a boy might take advantage sexually of young children. Actually, boys can be excellent baby-sitters; employing a girl doesn't automatically guarantee a child's safety. It is important to check carefully on anyone, boy or girl, who will be alone with children. Talk to them before you hire them and talk to other parents who have used them. Tell your children both the rules you expect them to follow while you're away and possible sitter behavior they shouldn't give in to—such as being told to do something they don't understand, being threatened, or being promised a special treat if they agree not to reveal a secret. Let the sitter know you always do this. Later take the trouble to ascertain how the child and the sitter get along. When children say they don't like someone, it's important to listen carefully and find out why this is.

Because so many cases of abuse in preschools and child care centers have come to light in recent years, many parents worry about their children's safety in such situations. The vast majority of these places are perfectly reputable, but recognizing parents' concern, the U.S. Department of Health and Human Services has put together a list of steps that parents can take to make sure their child is in a safe place during the day. These are their suggestions:

• Check with state or local licensing agencies, child care information or referral services, and other child care community agencies to make sure the program is reputable. Ask if there have been any complaints about it.
• Find out as much as possible about the teachers and care givers. Talk with parents whose children have been in the program for some time.
• Ask how the school or center selects its staff and whether it checks references and previous employment histories before hiring.
• Find out whether the school or center welcomes parent participation during the day. Take special note of the attitude toward having parents around.
• Make sure you have the right to drop in to visit at any time.
• Make sure you are informed about every planned outing. Never give the organization blanket permission to take your child off the premises. Prohibit, in writing, the release of your child to anyone without your explicit authorization. Make sure the program knows who will pick up your child on any given day.
• Go visiting unannounced every so often.

To this list, we add that children who leave home every day should know their whole name, their address, and telephone number. If they are too young to memorize the information, write it on a card and pin it to their clothing.

A convicted offender put his finger on how to prevent child molestation when he commented in a TV interview: "I can walk into a playground and at a glance pick out the child who will go with me. It's the one who needs more time with an

adult. Most adults don't see that." It is true that good communication between parents and children, coupled with early education about sexuality, provide the most effective protection
against sexual abuse of children.

WHEN A CHILD HAS BEEN ABUSED

The way parents respond to the fact of a sexual assault on
their child has a lot to do with the impact of the experience on
the girl or boy. The three most important things for parents to
do are to reassure the child that he or she did right to tell, that
he or she is in no way at fault for what happened, and that he
or she is still very much loved. If children expect that parents
won't believe them or that they will be angry or punitive, they
will very likely keep silent and carry the emotional scars from
the experience into adulthood. Incidentally, professionals who
work in the field of child abuse emphasize that it is something
children very rarely lie about. False reports of abuse are estimated at one in a hundred and these are almost never given by
younger children.

Besides believing, comforting, and reassuring the child who
has been molested, while making every effort to conceal their
own shock, anger, or disgust, there are other important steps
for parents to take. They should notify the police and a rape
crisis center or social services agency. If the abuse took place
in a school or day care center, they should not talk to personnel
there about it; let the authorities handle that. It is advisable to
have the child seen by an agency that helps sexual abuse victims with their strong feelings of shame and guilt and anger—a
hospital, child welfare agency, or community mental health
group. The child should also have a physical examination, preferably by a doctor who has the specialized training and sensitivity to carry it out without frightening the child. When this is
handled properly, it can reassure the child that his or her body
has not been changed, and that the harm is not permanent.
Expect a girl or boy who has been molested to show the effects

of the experience in various behavioral ways for quite some time.

If you suspect that your child has been abused, the best approach is to talk with the child. Comment, if the child is old enough to talk, that, for example, she seems more afraid of strangers (or whoever) than before . . . and ask if there is any reason. You might want to read, with your child, one of the excellent books mentioned in the resource section of this book. Sometimes reading together provides a "safe" way for a child to bring up a very scary topic. You might try one of the "what if . . ." games suggested earlier in this chapter. Your approach must depend on your child, your child's age, and your knowledge of what might have happened. More than likely, confrontational approaches such as "Did you let Mr. So-and-so get too close to you?" will not be helpful. Of course, if there is evidence of physical molestation or harm you should take the child for treatment and inform the doctor of your concern. Here, too, it is important to reassure your child that whatever happened was *not his or her fault* and that you are not angry with them. If a youngster has said nothing about being abused, but begins, inexplicably, to show behaviors mentioned below, it suggests strongly that he or she has had an extremely disturbing experience.

The behaviors that experts mention most often are listed below:

- Real changes in personality or behavior, regression to more infantile behavior like bed-wetting or thumb-sucking in young children. In older children fighting, exhibitionism, drug use, delinquency, running away are all indicators of possible sexual abuse.
- Nightmares, sleep disturbances, fear of the dark.
- Unusual interest in or knowledge of sexual matters; expressing affection in ways inappropriate for their age.
- Exaggerated fear of adults or of a particular adult; reluctance

to be left somewhere or with someone in particular; aversion to touch or closeness with anyone.
· Vaginal or rectal bleeding, itching, swollen genitals, vaginal infection, venereal disease.

DEALING WITH THE POSSIBILITY OF A DAUGHTER'S RAPE

The most common misconception about rape, as with child molestation, is that it is usually committed by a stranger. In fact, much more often the victim knows her attacker. According to the Department of Justice, "acquaintance rape" or "date rape" constitutes close to half of *reported* rape cases, and the majority of victims are between the ages of fifteen and twenty-four. Similarly, of the calls from victims to one representative rape crisis center in 1984, 75 percent of the callers knew their attacker and 35 percent were between thirteen and eighteen. It is not surprising then to read that in a 1982 study of male university students, 61 percent said they had touched a female sexually against her will.

Many boys say they don't consider it rape to force a date to have sex with them. But it is, and young girls are usually poorly equipped to prevent it. A combination of circumstances makes the average teenager especially vulnerable. She may not be sufficiently knowledgeable about sexuality to clearly recognize that verbal or physical pressure to have sex is abusive. She may believe she is "in love" when, in fact, she is only temporarily infatuated; she may think that compliance is expected of her or that it is the only way to keep the boy interested in her. She may also be afraid of her parents' anger if they find out that she has had intercourse.

Consider this example: A teenager accepts a date from an older male her parents have warned her against seeing. She has told them she'll be at her girlfriend's house for the evening. She and her date are parked on a lonely road ten miles from home when he makes his move. If she resists or jumps out of the car, how is she going to get home without letting her parents know she lied to them? Or perhaps her parents are away for the weekend and, in spite of their having expressly forbidden it, she invites her boyfriend in after a date and he decides to take advantage of the situation. He knows she can't tell her parents without getting into trouble.

In both cases, of course, the girl has not only disobeyed her parents but has shown poor judgment. That is small consolation in the face of rape. Parents have to expect that teenagers will disobey and use poor judgment sometimes—it is part of growing up.

Rather than assigning blame after the fact, it will be more productive if parents make sure their daughters understand that sex can be used in a variety of ways—to dominate and humiliate, as well as to express love or experience pleasure— so that they will be less vulnerable to, and better able to recognize, potential abuse. If girls have been given a clear set of values and a firm sense of their own worth since childhood, they will have the strength to defend themselves against exploitation.

Date rape is indefensible, although the double standard for male and female behavior that our society fosters frequently results in the downplaying of this type of abuse. If parents feel this is an unhealthy standard, they should bring their sons up to believe this and make sure their daughters are aware of it. Many boys, unfortunately, think they are supposed to press for sex, that girls secretly want to have it forced on them. Again because of the double standard, a common myth among teenagers is that a girl who is known to have had sex with one boy is available to every boy. If she doesn't agree to it, she deserves to be raped. Girls should also be told that a boy with a shaky sense of self-esteem himself can be sufficiently angered to commit rape by a refusal to have sex. Girls should be encouraged to be clear about their own wishes. Ambivalence or mixed messages are confusing to anyone, and may be even more so to an anxious and insecure young man.

Parents should let their children know that this kind of sexual assault can happen within the context of a "relationship," which in no way excuses it. If a couple have been "making out" for some time, the boy may suddenly decide he will not put up with any more frustration. Date rapes also take place when one or both of the teens have had too much to drink. Alcohol loosens inhibitions on the boy's part and may impair a girl's ability to resist.

Some practical tips for self-protection that parents might offer their youngsters are:

· Don't let a date you don't know well take you to a lonely, isolated spot.
· Realize that a boy's antennae are frequently up for sexual signals. If a girl doesn't know him well, she should make sure she doesn't do or say things he might interpret as come-ons.
· Girls should try to refuse unwanted advances as tactfully as possible. Don't make a boy feel you find him unattractive, or react in ways that will make him angry. But be assertive and consistent in saying no. Leave no room for doubt as to your sincerity.
· Don't assume that because a boy and girl are close, he may not use force at some time to make the girl have sex with him.
· There is no medical or physiological reason that a young man "has to have" sex.

A teenager who has been raped, whether by an acquaintance or by a stranger, feels ashamed, guilty, incompetent, stupid, and scared. If she knows the rapist, she is often unlikely to tell her parents what happened for fear of their disbelief, anger, or punishment. This is too bad, because she is in real need of help. She needs her parents to say, "We believe what you told us. It was not your fault that it happened, and we will help you in every way we can."

She would benefit by talking to experts at a rape crisis center, even if only on the telephone, about her feelings of shame and anger and her fear of bodily harm or of future sexual problems. Teenagers who have been assaulted once are at risk of its happening again. Their loss of self-esteem and their obvious vulnerability make them easy targets. The key to preventing this is counseling to break the pattern of behavior that makes them vulnerable. Parents themselves may also need to talk to a professional; the rape of one's child is deeply traumatic.

A girl who can't tell her parents in words may nonetheless behave in ways that suggest something deeply disturbing has happened to her. Any behavior that is unusual can be a clue—pronounced mood swings, unexplained weeping, withdrawal from friends or, on the other hand, seemingly compulsive sociability. Parents should try to steer a teenager showing such behavior to a trusted or trustworthy adult or to a professional counselor with whom she can talk about what happened to her.

Many victims have difficulty in deciding whether to report a rape, especially when the rapist is a friend or acquaintance. Rape is a crime, and should be reported to the police.

Whether or not the rape is reported, the victim should have a medical examination as soon as possible. The exam can determine whether there have been injuries other than the rape itself, test for STDs or pregnancy, and provide the medical evidence necessary to prosecute the perpetrator. During the medical exam the doctor will take a medical history, perform a physical exam, collect evidence (such as ripped clothing), take photographs, and provide medical or preventive treatment. The young woman has the right to refuse any part of the examination and to forbid the release of information to authorities.

A Planned Parenthood center or a rape crisis center will have the information needed to help the young woman and her family through the medical exam and, if she chooses, the police report. They can also refer for family counseling. Since most women of all ages experience rape with a horrible sense of emotional as well as physical violation and as loss of control over their lives, taking these steps to become a "survivor" instead of a victim can help her in her return to normal life. Parents should know that there is nothing they can do to make everything as it was, but that their love, care, and concern offer their child the best support.

CHAPTER 11

Sex and the Single Parent

Being a single parent isn't easy. As the mother of two grown children puts it, "It made my divorce look like a piece of cake. But the flip side is that once you have gotten through it, there isn't much left that can throw you." Never-married single mothers may not suffer the trauma of divorce or death of their children's father, but their situation as single head of a household is equally challenging.

Single parents learn quickly that they have to manage without the mutual support system that exists in most two-parent families. They have to get along with less earning power, less leisure, less companionship. They have to endure more loneliness, anxiety, and hardship. And even though they now make up one quarter of all American families, they still suffer from a lack of societal support as well. Socially in limbo, their situation surrounded by negative connotations, they are "going it alone" on a grand scale. Single divorced parents are a relatively new phenomenon. There are few accepted patterns of behavior for them. Traditional morals and manners handed down by earlier generations often do not apply.

When it comes to sexual relationships, they may be particularly vulnerable. Marriage partners don't have to explain their sexual or emotional needs to their children or anyone else—they come with the territory. Single parents, however, are faced with a direct challenge to examine their own feelings about sexuality.

This means that to achieve a satisfactory lifestyle for themselves and their children, they must at some point resolve the problem of how to be both the parents they want to be and the sexual persons they need to be. It's a tough problem.

When single parents talk to one another about their situation or ask for professional help, their concerns sound like these:

"I don't dare date till the divorce is final. I might lose custody of the children."

"Will it be really bad for my son if I let my lover stay overnight?"

"My son is rude to every date I bring home."

"My ex-wife won't let the children stay at my apartment because my girlfriend lives with me."

"My daughter's schoolmates make cracks about my having a boyfriend."

"The kids really resent my dating."

These are truly disturbing situations that married parents don't have to confront. Sometimes the guilt or anxiety associated with them is too much to handle. "I finally put my own needs on hold for ten years," a divorced mother told us. "I don't know whether it would be the right thing for everyone to do, but it was the only way I could be the kind of parent I wanted to be."

In fact, there is no one right or wrong way for single parents to handle their most significant relationships. What is right for one family may not be for another. And there is no equivalent of Miss Manners to lay down the rules. The only universally applicable standard is honesty.

The first and most positive step that single parents—divorced, widowed, or never married—can take is to confront their own sexuality honestly and become absolutely clear as to how their needs jibe with the values they want to impart to their children. As we've pointed out more than once, parents are the most powerful sexual influences their children have. What they say and, equally, what they do not say—their attitudes and their behavior—form the basis for the child's perception of sexual values. If what they are doing or what they are saying honestly feels all right to parents, it will feel the same to the child. If it doesn't feel right, if it makes them guilty or anxious, this is the message the child will get.

"I am very open with my children, who are four and eight, about the fact that I see and date several women," says a single father who is also a therapist. "And I haven't seen any evidence that they are frightened or upset by it."

By contrast, another divorced father of two little girls says he would not feel comfortable having women friends stay overnight when his daughters are visiting, nor would he feel right about staying over with women friends under the same circumstances. As a result, he has decided to cool it on sexual relationships for the time being.

Both of them are doing the appropriate thing—for their particular families.

Single parents of adolescent children face a more complex situation than those whose offspring are still young: "How can I preach one thing and practice another?"

If parents were brought up to believe that sexual activity should be reserved for marriage, they may feel they should urge their teenagers to follow that course. This may be the case even when the parent no longer accepts this moral standard for himself. Again, one solution that won't fill the parent with either guilt or frustration is honesty. Admit there is a double standard. What may be appropriate behavior for an adult is not appropriate for an unmarried adolescent. Your child may not agree with you, but your honesty will make a deeper impression than demands for compliance or attempts to deny that you have sexual needs.

A parent's divorce or separation or death is deeply unnerving to most children. It has profound effects on their feelings about their own lives and their relationships with their parents. Recognizing the powerful emotions that are driving their children and understanding their origins can help parents make the transition to a new kind of family more successful.

Children crave stability in their lives. It spells safety. The breakup of an apparently stable family makes them feel terribly helpless and imperiled. When two households must be maintained instead of one, living standards for both may go down; children may be uprooted from a familiar home; the parent they live with may have less time and attention to give to them just when they need more.

So it should not be surprising if children overreact either negatively or positively to any man or woman who seems to be replacing the absent parent. They can't help but resent someone they feel is taking up the time and attention they so desperately need. Often they fantasize that their parents will reconcile, and any new "friend" of either is a threat to that fantasy. Or they may need a replacement for the absent parent so badly that they try to attach themselves to any substitute.

One of the first things single parents need to do if they are going to keep the family on an even keel is to convince children that their relationship with Mother or Father is not diminished, that they are no less loved or attended to. This isn't always easy for a person distracted by new situations, anxieties, and problems. One way to make children feel more secure is to set up with them a special time every day, time that is devoted exclusively to that particular child. Parent and child plan together what they will do in that time, and nothing is allowed to interrupt it. If a child *knows* that the parent is focusing some special time for him alone, then he may feel less threatened if the single parent begins to see a new adult who is also claiming time.

Making sure in words and deeds that your children know that you will always have time for them, and that you value and love them, may reduce the hostile reactions single parents sometimes get when they introduce a new friend.

"What can I do about how horribly rude my children are to anyone I bring home?" divorced parents often ask family counselors. As well as the background preparation we discussed above, it will be useful to try to uncover the cause of the behavior rather than simply to respond to it. Are the children angry about something specific? Are they afraid? Are their feelings hurt? Try to get them to talk about, and think about, why they are behaving as they are and see what you can do to make them feel less hostile—short of giving up your friend. Sometimes parents unthinkingly add to the overload of anxiety children of divorce are living with. "How would you feel if one of your parents said he or she was going out for a little while in the evening and didn't come home till the next day?" a teenager points out.

It makes most children uncomfortable to think about their parents as sexual beings. They most often think about them as old and sexless. Married couples usually make an effort not to upset that image. It is not as easy for single parents to be discreet about their sexual activity, but it may be worth attempting. Those who seem to have managed their new family life most successfully say they were careful not to expose their children to every casual date or to a succession of "sleepover friends." When they developed a significant relationship with one particular person, they introduced that person into the household gradually, tactfully, and considerately.

An issue between many divorced couples is that they have different—possibly opposed—sets of sexual values, and each worries about what the other is exposing the children to. Often the conflicts center, not around the children's behavior, but around the behavior of the other parent. It may be very difficult for one parent to avoid angry or judgmental statements about the behavior of the other. If there is any communication at all between ex-couples in this situation, they should jointly recognize that such attitudes simply upset and confuse their children.

It's best if divorced parents can, for the good of their children, agree to disagree. One way to do this might be to say, "Those are the rules at your father's house; these are the rules here."

As we have said several times in this book, children learn their values partly by the way their parents and other important adults in their lives react to the behavior of others, as well as by being "taught" values and observing others' behavior.

It is particularly necessary for single parents to start working early on the sexual values they want their children to grow up with. It's the best way they have to influence the behavior of teenagers who will have to make decisions independently of their parents.

"One of the hardest things I had to deal with when I got divorced and went back to work," a mother says, "was knowing that if the girls decided to disobey me and invite boys home from school in the afternoon, there really wasn't any way I could stop them."

In fact, some of the most painful conflicts between parents and offspring arise when there are adolescent children in the family.

The breakup of a marriage has a somewhat different impact on children at different ages. For adolescents, who are at a growth stage that makes them particularly preoccupied with relationships, it can be particularly severe. Drs. Judith Wallerstein and Joan Kelly, who have studied in depth the effects of divorce on children, say that the threat a divorce poses to adolescents lies in its effect on normal developmental processes.

In a stable family, be it with one or two parents, teens disengage psychologically from their parents over an extended period of time, taking a few steps toward maturity and independence and then falling back periodically into more childish dependence. While this is going on, their perception of parents is gradually developing from one of childish awe through typical disenchantment to a realistic view of them as human beings. In the process of moving out to maturity, adolescents have an especially strong need for a family structure that will both support and control them.

When the family breaks up, all these developmental processes are interfered with and the time allowed for growing up is dramatically foreshortened. To the child, the parents often seem to have changed and to be acting childishly themselves. They become preoccupied with their own lives and less available; the support of the family structure has been toppled. As one thirteen-year-old girl said to Drs. Wallerstein and Kelly, "I felt like I was being thrown out in the world before I was ready."

The evident sexual behavior of their single parents is also bothersome to adolescents and can produce feelings that include sexual excitement, acute anxiety, anger, outrage, embarrassment, dismay, and envy.

A young person may feel that if her *mother* can date and have intercourse, she can too. Unfortunately, at times, these feelings can result in a type of sexual competition, especially if parents become involved with partners closer in age to their children than to themselves. Daughter flirts with Mother's new friend, or son with Father's new friend, or the mother shows the teenager that she is still attractive, even to the daughter's friends. One divorced mother, looking back on the period soon after her divorce, ruefully commented, "I was the world's oldest teenager for a while there."

The result very often is sexual behavior on the part of their children that parents find dismaying. The researchers explain why: unless adolescent boys and girls have developed the inner control, good judgment, and sound conscience they need to replace parental control and guidance, they feel especially vulnerable to their new sexual and aggressive impulses and to the temptations of the adolescent world. A number of studies have shown that teenage girls in one-parent homes have a higher likelihood of being sexually active than those in two-parent homes. One particular study, of sixty-eight divorcing families, showed that in the first year after the divorce the incidence of sexual "acting out" by teenage children increased.

Since this sexual "acting out" can be the teenager's way of expressing feelings like anger, loneliness, jealousy, outrage, or a sense of abandonment, the most fruitful way for parents to deal with it is to try to get at the cause and correct that if they can or, at the least, acknowledge its existence in frank talks with the child. Whenever possible, being more available and more supportive may help prevent self-damaging sexual activity on the part of the child.

Being a single parent, you may be confronted more often with the challenge to examine your own attitudes and your own sexual behavior, so that you can honestly deal with your children's needs. This is not necessarily a bad thing. You may have a chance, especially with a teenager, to open discussions on topics that parents in two-parent households find very difficult to tackle. Discussions of feelings of attraction, love, and decision making may be given a new immediacy by your own situation. We, along with those who are professionals in the field of divorce counseling, do caution you to distinguish between sharing your feelings and using your child as your "best friend." Expecting your child, who may seem exceptionally mature, to help you deal with your emotional problems is giving the child an unneeded burden.

In sum, single parenting need not make talking with your child about sex and sexuality more difficult. Single mothers can and should talk to both their sons and their daughters, just as in two-parent households. Divorced fathers can and should talk to both their sons and daughters about sex and sexuality. Children can in this way have two, sometimes very different, perspectives on human sexuality and their own behavior— both from people who are very important to them, and who have their best interests at heart. In this world of many and conflicting media messages about sex, to gain two such perspectives may in fact help children deal with conflicting messages from their peers, and from the media.

CHAPTER 12

Sex and the Latchkey Child

"Latchkey children" are boys and girls who go home from school to an empty house because the parent or parents they live with are at work. The term was coined early in the nineteenth century and in the 1940s began to be used to describe the children who wore housekeys on strings around their necks. Not too many years ago, leaving subteen children at home alone was considered something responsible parents just didn't do. Today, highly responsible parents are doing it in ever increasing numbers. It is an inevitable spin-off of our present society and economy. More than two million children between the ages of seven and thirteen spend the afternoon hours alone or with siblings.

Since the latchkey explosion began, many parents and child care professionals have worried about the effects of the experience on children's development. Judging by the few studies that have been undertaken, when parents lay the proper groundwork and their children are emotionally mature enough to handle the situation, the increased responsibility need not create a problem and can even be useful.

This doesn't mean, however, that there are no risks aside from physical safety to watch out for. In surveys that ask teenagers where they had intercourse, the most frequent answer is the home of one of the partners or another friend's home. In our society, where nearly all single parents must work and where, in most two-parent households, both parents work, there is always at least one young person in a group of friends whose house is "adult-free" in the afternoons. Parents who do work outside the home should have a realistic appraisal of some of the possible influences on their child's sexual behavior during their daily absence.

Children who feel they lack in nurturance or emotional support when they reach adolescence may try to satisfy those needs through sexual activity. They may also be expressing resentment by having intercourse, contrary to their parents' expressed values. One young woman who had been a latchkey child from the age of seven until she went away to college told us how much she resented it. At thirteen she started asking boys over in the afternoons and going to bed with them. "I was trying to force my mother to stay home to control me," she says, looking back on the experience.

Staying home alone every afternoon instead of playing with other children can make boys and girls slow to develop social skills. In adolescence they may see sex as the only way to relate to their peers.

Sexual advances from older brothers to younger sisters with whom they spend every afternoon alone are not unheard of. Because a little sister is almost always reluctant to tell on an older sibling, she should be questioned thoughtfully if she suddenly becomes reluctant to stay alone with him. The family will need to seek professional help if the child has indeed been abused. (See the chapter on protecting children from abuse.)

Television can replace parents as the most important source of information with unfortunate results. When the TV is a child's *only* companion for several after-school hours, the possibility of negative results are increased. As the American Academy of Pediatrics (AAP) pointed out in a 1984 policy statement: "The portrayal of sex roles and sexuality on television is unrealistic and misleading; sexual relationships develop rapidly; the risk of pregnancy is rarely considered; adolescence is portrayed as a constant state of sexual crisis. These characteristics may contribute directly or indirectly to the risk of adolescent pregnancy and clearly alter age-dependent experimental learning with respect to sexuality." Among other recommendations, the AAP would like to see it become technologically possible for parents to "alter or control their children's viewing habits."

To make sure their children don't become sexual casualties because of a latchkey upbringing, parents can consider the following steps:

1. Begin sex education and the teaching of sexual values early. Their acceptance of your values is the major influence you can have on your children's behavior when you are not around.

2. Lay down the rules about TV watching in the afternoon as soon as children start being at home alone. Sex and violence shows are by no means limited to evening hours. TV can be a useful teaching tool if an adult is present to interpret the situations it depicts. It can also, as the American Academy of Pediatrics points out, be disastrously misleading without such guidance.

3. Give them a structure to work within—starting dinner, etc., walking the dog, setting the table, or some tasks which are theirs to do.

4. Try to work out some form of age-appropriate supervision for at least part of a child's after-school time. Community support for latchkey families is beginning to grow. In many communities after-school programs are sponsored by youth groups, city recreation departments, community neighborhood centers, libraries, schools, churches, and other groups. Some large cities like New York have excellent settlement house programs that run five days a week

and are also open during school holidays and in vacation periods.

5. Encourage children to express their feelings about the latchkey arrangement. Make sure they understand why it is necessary. Find out if they are lonely or frightened and see if there is a way to minimize those feelings. If they feel deprived, try to find ways to compensate for your absence in the after-school hours by spending the time you do have together creatively.

6. Be choosy about which friends a child may have over in the afternoon and how many at a time. Some parents make it a rule from the beginning that opposite-sex friends are allowed to visit only when they are home so they will not have to change the rules when adolescence and potential problems loom.

7. Be honest with teens about your concerns for them. They resent having limits imposed on their freedom without explanations. A reasonable answer for a daughter who wants to know why she can't have boys over after school is, "I don't want to run the risk of your getting into a situation you can't handle."

8. If a latchkey arrangement is the one you make for your child, don't torture yourself with guilt about it. A recent study conducted at the University of North Carolina compared a group of self-care children with one under adult supervision and found no differences between them in self-esteem, internal control, or social adjustment and interpersonal relations. When the latchkey arrangement is well handled, it helps young people learn useful skills, solve problems, and learn to take on responsibility. It can have as many pluses as minuses.

Ultimately, all parents must "love and let go." For parents who work outside the home, and whose children take care of themselves in the afternoons, some of the "letting go" may come at an earlier age.

In this book, we have held all along that it is important to begin helping your child learn about sex and sexuality from birth, by your actions as well as with your words. Those of us who are working parents have a special responsibility to help our children develop values and be able to act on those values independently. With this kind of learning and with our loving support, children have a good start at growing into loving, caring adults.

Afterword

In the summer of 1985, PPFA commissioned a national public opinion survey from Louis Harris and Associates. We found a high degree of concern about the teenage pregnancy problem. Most people understand that the solutions lie in increased communication and information and better acc 3s to birth control services. We also found a high level of support for sexuality education programs in the public schools, for inclusion of messages about birth control on television, and for laws that would require schools to establish links with family planning clinics to educate youngsters about family planning and to offer them access to contraceptives. We saw a desire for a more open climate about sex.

Planned Parenthood has made the reduction of unintended births to teenagers a national goal of the organization. Attaining this goal requires the cooperation of all parts of our society. Parents, as the first and primary sexuality educators for their children, are key to helping their children understand the family's values about sexuality.

When or if you want more assistance in this important task, there are Planned Parenthood educators at all our affiliates who will be glad to help.

Appendices

A Glossary of Sexual Terms*

ABORTION—See TERMINATION OF PREGNANCY.

ABSTINENCE—refraining from SEXUAL INTERCOURSE.

ADOLESCENCE—also called PUBERTY. Usually begins at age nine or ten in girls, at age ten or later in boys, and may continue through the teens. This is the time when girls and boys start to notice certain changes in their bodies and emotions. These changes, triggered by HORMONES, mean that girls and boys will soon become mature women and men. Changes in girls include breasts getting bigger and hips getting wider. Organs making up the reproductive system also mature and start working. These organs are the OVARIES, UTERUS, CERVIX, VAGINA, and FALLOPIAN TUBES. During this time, an adolescent girl also starts to MENSTRUATE.

Boys also notice body changes. The voice deepens, shoulders broaden, and hair appears on the face and other parts of the body. The PENIS, TESTICLES, and SCROTUM grow larger. During this time, a boy usually starts to make SPERM

* This glossary is compiled from Planned Parenthood publications and summarizes the definitions developed by the American College of Obstetricians and Gynecologists.

and EJACULATE. This happens because his male HOR-
MONES are working. Most boys and girls have dreams or
fantasize about sex. Sometimes when a boy is having a sexy
dream, he may have an ERECTION and may EJACULATE.
Girls also have sexy dreams, but they don't ejaculate at CLI-
MAX, as boys do. When a girl becomes sexually excited, her
VAGINA becomes moist with a lubrication fluid. Having sexy
dreams and fantasies and becoming sexually excited is a
normal part of growing up.

During PUBERTY both boys and girls begin to grow hair
under the arms and in the PUBIC AREA. Body odor also
becomes stronger, so it's important to keep clean. Each boy
and girl is an individual and develops at his or her own rate.

BREASTS—both women and men have breasts. However, a
woman's breasts grow larger than a man's during PUBERTY
and can produce milk after childbirth. The size of a woman's
breasts has nothing to do with her ability to feed a newborn.
Breasts also are a source of sexual pleasure in most women
and some men.

CERVIX—this is the lower part of the UTERUS. It has a small
opening into the VAGINA. This small hole (cervical opening)
lets the menstrual fluid or PERIOD come out; it also lets a
man's SPERM CELLS travel into the UTERUS and FALLO-
PIAN TUBES. During CHILDBIRTH the cervical opening can
also stretch wide enough to let a baby pass through. After
childbirth the cervix shrinks down to its normal size.

CHILDBIRTH—the process in which a baby is pushed out of
the woman's UTERUS and VAGINA after it has developed
enough to live outside on its own. The period of development
inside the uterus is called PREGNANCY and takes about
nine months.

CIRCUMCISION—this is a simple surgical procedure that
removes the loose skin (foreskin) which covers the end of the
PENIS. It's usually done when a baby boy is a newborn. If a

boy or man is not circumcised, special care needs to be taken to clean the area under the loose skin to avoid unpleasant odor and possible infection.

CLIMAX—also known as orgasm, or "coming." For both women and men, climax usually happens at the peak of SEXUAL INTERCOURSE or MASTURBATION. There is a feeling of pleasure that ranges from mild to very pleasurable. When a man reaches climax, SEMEN containing SPERM spurts out of the end of the PENIS. After climax the man loses his ERECTION and the penis goes back to its normal soft state. Women do not spurt out fluid the way a man does, but the VAGINA collects a liquid which acts as "lubrication" during sexual excitement. A woman can get pregnant whether or not she has a climax during sexual intercourse.

CLITORIS—this is a small, sensitive organ about the size of a pea. It's located in the soft folds of the skin that meet just above the VAGINA and URETHRA. It has many nerve endings and is very sensitive. Pleasurable feelings result when the clitoris is touched during lovemaking, SEXUAL INTERCOURSE, or MASTURBATION. Stimulating the clitoris is the main way most women reach a climax.

CONCEPTION—when a woman's EGG CELL unites with a man's SPERM CELL, FERTILIZATION occurs. Fertilization occurs almost always in the FALLOPIAN TUBE. After fertilization the "fertilized egg" starts to divide until it is a tiny ball of cells. Then it travels through a fallopian tube to the UTERUS. If it attaches (implants) itself to the wall of the uterus, conception occurs, and PREGNANCY is said to have begun.

CONDOM—this is a man's method of CONTRACEPTION. It's a sheath of thin rubber or animal tissue. Condoms can be purchased one at a time or in packages; they come rolled up. A condom is put on by unrolling it over the erect PENIS before SEXUAL INTERCOURSE. When the man EJACU-

LATES, the condom acts like a bag and catches the SPERM so it can't enter the woman's VAGINA. The condom is very effective when used the right way; effectiveness increases when the woman inserts FOAM into the VAGINA at the same time a man uses a condom. Condoms can be easily purchased from drugstores; no prescription is necessary.

CONTRACEPTION—this is often another word used for most of the various methods of "birth control." Contraception is a method used to prevent a man's SPERM CELL from entering a woman's EGG CELL and beginning a PREGNANCY. Methods of contraception include: CONDOM, DIAPHRAGM, IUD, "THE PILL," FERTILITY AWARENESS METHODS (FAM), and VAGINAL CONTRACEPTIVES which include foam, jellies, creams, and suppositories. STERILIZATION is called permanent contraception. Withdrawal and douching should not be considered methods of contraception.

DIAPHRAGM—this looks like a shallow cup and is made of soft rubber with a firm rim. It's used with contraceptive cream or jelly. A woman puts it into her VAGINA before SEXUAL INTERCOURSE. The diaphragm covers the opening to the UTERUS so the SPERM CELL can't enter. The contraceptive cream or jelly acts to stop the sperm's movement. Just about any woman can use a diaphragm. However, since a woman needs to have it individually fitted, a prescription is necessary.

EJACULATION—when a man has a CLIMAX, a whitish liquid spurts from the end of the PENIS. This is called ejaculate, and the liquid is called SEMEN. A man ejaculates and urinates from the same opening. However, the body shuts off urination when a man ejaculates, so semen and urine cannot mix and come out at the same time during climax.

ERECTION—a man's PENIS swells, gets hard and erect when he's sexually excited. A man can get an erection if the penis is touched, or rubbed, or while thinking about sex or having a sexually exciting dream. An erection goes away slowly by itself or quicker if a man EJACULATES. An erection is caused by veins in the PENIS filling up with blood. Even male babies have erections, but the strong feelings related to sex do not usually happen until PUBERTY.

EGG CELL—this is a woman's reproductive cell. A mature egg cell is half of what it takes to start a pregnancy; the other half is provided by a man's SPERM CELL. A woman is born with all the eggs she'll ever have; they're contained in her OVARIES. At PUBERTY the ovaries start to work and a mature egg is released at the rate of about once a month. An egg cell is so small it can be seen only with a microscope.

FALLOPIAN TUBES—two muscular passages that transport EGG CELLS from the OVARIES to the UTERUS.

FERTILE—a woman is fertile or is able to get pregnant just before, during, and just after an OVARY releases an EGG CELL. When a girl starts to menstruate, she usually starts releasing an egg cell about once a month; this means she can get pregnant. When a boy starts having EJACULATIONS, his TESTICLES are making SPERM CELLS, and he can make a girl pregnant.

FERTILITY AWARENESS METHODS (FAM)—Natural Family Planning, Sympto-Thermal Method, Ovulation Method, Mucus/Temperature, Rhythm are all different names for one or more methods that are used to figure out when a woman is likely to be FERTILE (able to get pregnant) each month. FAM is a word used to describe these methods or combinations of methods.

By trying to pinpoint her fertile days, she can avoid having sex on those days or can use some form of CONTRACEPTION, thereby preventing pregnancy. However, this is not as easy as it may sound because determining the fertile days depends on knowing the exact day a woman will release an egg. See OVULATION.

There are several methods. One involves checking the discharge (mucus) in the VAGINA daily. Another means keeping a record of body temperature every day. Still another involves keeping a daily calendar record of menstrual periods.

These methods require time, effort, and keeping careful records. To make one or a combination of these methods work best, a woman should talk to someone who has experience with these methods, or should take a class in FAM.

FERTILIZATION—if a SPERM CELL enters, or unites with, a woman's EGG CELL, fertilization happens. The "fertilized" egg starts to divide and grow as it travels down a connecting FALLOPIAN TUBE to the UTERUS. Only one sperm cell is needed to fertilize an egg cell.

FOAM—this is one type of VAGINAL CONTRACEPTIVE. It's inserted into the VAGINA before each act of SEXUAL INTERCOURSE. Foam contains a chemical that destroys SPERM so they can't swim upward toward the UTERUS. It also acts as a barrier to keep sperm from entering a woman's uterus. The chemical won't hurt the vaginal tissue. Used consistently and correctly, foam is relatively effective. Greater protection is possible if a man uses a CONDOM at the same time a woman uses foam. This is not a prescription method. It can be purchased in drugstores; directions on how to use it are in each package.

GENITALS—this is another word for external sex organs. In males, genitals include the PENIS, TESTICLES, and SCROTUM. In females, they include the VULVA (the soft folds of skin around a woman's vagina), the VAGINA itself, and the CLITORIS.

HETEROSEXUAL—a person who has sex with, and feels romantic love for, people of the opposite sex.

HOMOSEXUAL—a person who has sex with, and feels romantic love for, people of the same sex. Sometimes girls and boys "get a crush" on someone of the same sex when they're teenagers. These feelings are normal and have nothing to do with whether a boy or girl is, or will be, homosexual ("gay") or HETEROSEXUAL ("straight") when they're adults. Usually these feelings of affection are for a favorite teacher or a good friend they admire. Nobody knows for sure why some people are homosexual or heterosexual.

HORMONES—these are substances made by the body. They're triggered by a center in the brain. Hormones act like messengers and tell certain glands and organs what to do. Special hormones, called sex hormones, cause the body changes that happen during PUBERTY. They also tell the reproductive parts of the body to start working.

IUD—short for "IntraUterine Device." This is a small device usually made of plastic. It's put inside a woman's UTERUS by a clinician (a doctor or nurse practitioner). One way the IUD works is to hinder a pregnancy from occurring by keeping the fertilized egg from attaching to the lining of the UTERUS. IUDs come in various shapes and types. Some can be left in indefinitely; others have to be replaced at a specific time, varying from one to three years. If a woman wants to become pregnant, she has the IUD removed by a clinician. IUDs may no longer be available in the United States.

LABIA—the inner and outer folds (lips) that surround the opening of the VAGINA.

MASTURBATION—this refers to rubbing or touching the sex organs to cause pleasurable feelings or a CLIMAX. Masturbation is considered normal. No bad effects happen to people who masturbate. It won't make a person get sick, go crazy, or use up SPERM CELLS.

MENOPAUSE—this is the time of life when a woman's OVARIES stop making HORMONES and releasing eggs and she gradually stops menstruating completely. This usually happens between the ages of forty-five and fifty-five, but depends on the individual. After menopause, when a woman stops having PERIODS for six months or more, she is no longer FERTILE. She can still enjoy sex; she just can't get pregnant.

MENSTRUATION—about once a month, an OVARY releases an EGG. The egg then travels down a connecting FALLOPIAN TUBE toward the UTERUS. At the same time the uterus starts building up a lining or "nest" of extra tissue and blood to nourish a possible PREGNANCY. If pregnancy does not happen, the lining isn't needed. So it's shed and comes out of the VAGINA. This is called the menstrual flow, or PERIOD. Most women menstruate anywhere from every twenty-one to thirty-two days. A period generally lasts from three to seven days.

OVARIES—these are two glands; one (called an ovary) is located on each side of the UTERUS. Ovaries contain EGG CELLS and make female HORMONES (estrogen and progesterone) that regulate the menstrual cycle. A female is born with all the egg cells she will ever have in her lifetime. A woman starts releasing egg cells sometime during PUBERTY at the rate of about once a month.

OVULATION—this means that an OVARY releases a ripe EGG CELL to be picked up by a connecting FALLOPIAN TUBE. If the egg cell does not unite with a SPERM CELL, pregnancy does not happen. When a woman is not pregnant, MENSTRUATION occurs about fourteen days after ovulation because the built-up uterine lining is not needed.

Any woman using FAM should know that she is considered FERTILE (able to get pregnant) shortly before, during, and for a few days after ovulation. The reason a woman must know she is about to become fertile *before* ovulation is that a man's SPERM can live in her body up to five days. Suppose a woman has unprotected intercourse on Monday and releases an egg on Friday. The sperm may still be alive and unite with the egg she releases on Friday. As soon as an egg is *released*, it can be fertilized within hours. And *after* ovulation, a woman remains fertile because her egg can live for two or three days. That's why it's so important to try to determine the exact day of ovulation.

OVUM—another word for an EGG CELL. More than one ovum are called ova.

PENIS—this is one of the male's sex organs. When the veins in the penis are filled with blood during sexual excitement, the man has an ERECTION. During SEXUAL INTERCOURSE, the man puts his penis into the woman's VAGINA. The penis is very sensitive to sexual feelings. A man EJACULATES and urinates from the end of his penis, but not at the same time.

PERIOD—this is sometimes used as another word for menstrual flow. A normal period may last from three to seven days. It usually comes out of the VAGINA slowly; it shouldn't spurt or gush. During the first few days, the flow will usually be heaviest. Then it becomes less and less, until it stops completely. Young girls who have just started to menstruate may sometimes skip periods until their bodies get adjusted. However, if a girl is sexually active and misses a period, the most common cause is pregnancy.

"THE PILL"—this is an oral contraceptive; it's a prescription method taken by mouth. When a woman is on "the pill," she takes a series of pills every month; it's important to stay on schedule and not skip any. They're made of substances similar to the hormones produced by a woman's body. Generally they act to keep the ovaries from releasing eggs. The pill is the most effective method of temporary CONTRACEPTION. However, not all women should take the pill. Some women may have health problems or conditions that make the pill unsuitable. That's why it's necessary to have a physical exam beforehand. Regular checkups are necessary if the pill is prescribed.

PREGNANCY—happens as a result of SEXUAL INTERCOURSE. When an EGG CELL is fertilized, it travels down a connecting FALLOPIAN TUBE toward the UTERUS and then attaches (implants) itself to the wall of the uterus. There it starts to divide and grow. At this point pregnancy is said to have begun. A pregnancy takes about nine months.

PROSTATE GLAND—this is one of several male glands. It produces fluid that mixes with SPERM to form SEMEN, which is ejaculated by a male at the time of climax.

PUBERTY—refers to the time of life when the bodies of both boys and girls start to change as they mature into adults. The changes include physical growth, sexual development, and emotional changes. See ADOLESCENCE.

PUBIC AREA—the area between the legs in both women and men where the external genital organs are located. It's covered with "pubic hair" that starts to grow at PUBERTY.

RHYTHM METHOD—See FERTILITY AWARENESS METHODS (FAM).

SCROTUM—this looks like a sack hanging behind the PENIS: the scrotum holds the TESTICLES. Testicles need to be kept at a temperature that's not too hot or too cold so they can make SPERM CELLS. When it's warm, the scrotum gets a little larger to expose more skin to keep the testicles cool. When it's cold, the scrotum shrinks up close to the body to save heat.

SEMEN—this is the whitish fluid that comes out of the end of a man's PENIS when he EJACULATES. Semen contains SPERM CELLS and other body fluids. Each sperm cell is so tiny it can be seen only with a microscope.

SEMINAL VESICLES—these are two small sacs located near the PROSTATE. They serve to store SEMEN temporarily.

SEXUAL INTERCOURSE—this refers to the man putting his erect PENIS into a woman's VAGINA. Their physical movements produce sexual pleasure. If the man ejaculates SPERM, it's possible for one to combine with an EGG and cause PREGNANCY unless CONTRACEPTION is used.

STDs—refers to infections that happen in the sex organs. There are many types of infections; today they're all being referred to as STDs, which stands for SEXUALLY TRANSMISSIBLE DISEASES. Many people get infections in their sex organs during their lifetime. Some are more dangerous to a person's health than others. Some can happen without having sex. But all can be given or "transmitted" when there's close physical contact during sex. That's why they are more often referred to as STDs instead of venereal disease.

There are some things that should be remembered about STDs. Each infection has its own treatment, but you have to see a doctor to tell what kind it is and how to treat it. You can't get immune to STDs; you can get the same infection again.

Syphilis, gonorrhea, and herpes are more serious STDs. Common signs are sores and blisters in the genital area, an unusual discharge from the genitals, or rashes or bumps in the genital area and other parts of the body. A burning pain may be noticed during urination.

Some Precautions: using CONDOMS or a VAGINAL CONTRACEPTIVE during SEXUAL INTERCOURSE helps prevent infections from spreading. Having sexual contact with one person only, who is not having sexual contact with others, helps cut down on risk. Washing the GENITALS right before and after contact also helps reduce risk, but an infection could spread before soap and water reaches it.

The best rule is: don't take chances. If you suspect you've

had contact with someone who has STD, or you have symptoms that could be STD, see a doctor or go to a medical clinic right away. Minors in most states can be tested and treated for STD without telling their parents.

SPERM CELLS—these are tiny male reproductive cells that are made in the TESTICLES. When a man EJACULATES, he spurts out SEMEN which contains 100 to 300 million sperm cells. Sperm cells have tails that help them swim. If a man ejaculates inside the woman's VAGINA, the sperm cells swim up through her UTERUS and into the tubes. If a sperm cell finds, and enters, a woman's EGG CELL in her tubes, FERTILIZATION occurs. Sperm cells can live in a woman's body for three to five days. Boys start making sperm cells sometime during ADOLESCENCE.

STERILIZATION—this is a surgical procedure a man or a woman may choose to have if a firm decision has been made that no children or no more children are wanted. The operation blocks the SPERM-carrying tubes in a man or the EGG-carrying tubes in a woman. Only one partner needs to have the operation. The sex organs that account for maleness and femaleness are not touched. After the operation, a woman cannot get pregnant; a man cannot become a father. It is intended to be permanent and is considered better than 99 percent effective.

TERMINATION OF PREGNANCY—this is another name for "induced abortion," which is one kind of abortion. The other kind is called "spontaneous abortion," or miscarriage.

Induced abortion is a surgical procedure done by a licensed physician when a woman decides she must end a pregnancy for medical or personal reasons. The type of procedure depends on how far along the pregnancy is. There are risks with any surgical procedure. However, induced abortion done in the early months of pregnancy is considered relatively simple. Even induced abortions done in the later months of pregnancy also are relatively safe. Induced abortion is legal in the United States since a Supreme Court decision in January 1973. Induced abortion should not be substituted for the use of CONTRACEPTION.

The other kind of abortion is called "spontaneous abortion," or a miscarriage. This happens when the natural body processes end pregnancy before birth—usually before the twenty-fifth week of pregnancy. Miscarriage, or "spontaneous abortion," is sometimes nature's way of indicating something is wrong with the developing fetus, such as a birth defect or deformities.

TESTICLES—two glands located inside the SCROTUM. These glands make the SPERM CELLS and a male hormone called testosterone. The testicles start making sperm cells sometime during ADOLESCENCE and continue until old age. One testicle may hang lower than the other; this is normal.

URETHRA—the opening from which either a man or woman urinates. In the male it is at the end of the PENIS. Sometimes men get infections in the urethra. If it hurts to urinate, a boy or man should be checked by a doctor.

In the female the urethra is located between the opening of the VAGINA and CLITORIS.

UTERUS—(also called the womb). This is a pear-shaped organ located at the top of the VAGINA. It holds the developing fetus when a woman is pregnant. The uterus stretches to hold the growing fetus, then shrinks down to normal size after birth. The lining of the uterus is shed about once a month (MENSTRUATION) if a woman doesn't get pregnant.

VAGINA—this is an elastic passage in a woman that leads from the external sex organs (between her legs) to the UTERUS. The vagina can stretch to hold a tampon to soak up the menstrual flow, and it stretches wide enough to let a baby out at birth. The vagina also holds a man's PENIS during SEXUAL INTERCOURSE.

VAGINAL CONTRACEPTIVES—can take the form of FOAM, jellies, creams, suppositories. These are contraceptive products that can be purchased from the drugstore without a prescription. They are packaged in different ways. Foam usually comes in an aerosol container, jelly comes in a tube, and suppositories look like little pellets. Vaginal contraceptives need to be inserted into the VAGINA before each act of SEXUAL INTERCOURSE. They are intended to prevent PREGNANCY with a chemical that destroys SPERM. They also form a barrier over the CERVIX.

VAS DEFERENS—refers to the tubes that carry SPERM CELLS from the TESTICLES to the PENIS.

VD—this stands for venereal disease (See SEXUALLY TRANSMISSIBLE DISEASE).

VULVA—the outside of the VAGINA made up of soft folds of skin called "lips" or "labia." During puberty when a girl's body starts to develop, hair begins to grow on the vulva; this is called pubic hair. Hair also grows under the arms.

WET DREAMS—when a male has sexy dreams at night leading to sexual excitement, EJACULATION often happens. This is the body's way of relieving sexual tension and is considered normal. Women also have sexy dreams that can lead to CLIMAX. However, women do not ejaculate. During sexual excitement, a woman's VAGINA gets moist with a lubricating fluid.

WITHDRAWAL—this means that during SEXUAL INTERCOURSE the man "pulls out" his PENIS from the woman's VAGINA before EJACULATION. This is not considered a reliable method of CONTRACEPTION for two reasons. It's very difficult to do and puts a strain on both partners because the natural impulse is to thrust deeper into the vagina during sexual pleasure. Another reason this method is not reliable is because some SPERM may leak out of the PENIS before CLIMAX and swim into the UTERUS and tubes to start a PREGNANCY.

Facts About Methods of Contraception

This information is given so you will understand the different methods that you can use to prevent pregnancy. Some work better than others. The only way that works 100 percent is to say "no." Different people have different needs and lifestyles. So consider how important preventing pregnancy is to you and how suitable a particular method might be for you and your partner. Be sure to ask your clinician any questions you may have.

Some methods need to be medically prescribed. The birth control pill, the intrauterine device, and the diaphragm give quite reliable protection against pregnancy when used according to instructions. But not all of these methods are good for all women. Whether any one of these can be used is based on information about each woman's past and present health, plus a physical examination. Such a physical examination is recommended at least once a year, particularly if one of the above methods is used.

THE PILL

What this is: A monthly series of birth control pills. The ingredients are similar to hormones normally produced in a woman's body.

What this does: Most kinds of birth control pills keep the ovaries from releasing eggs. They do this only if taken regularly for the full monthly series. If one or more pills are forgotten, pregnancy may happen.

How well this works*: Of one hundred women on the pill, about two may become pregnant during the first year of actual use. Women who never forget the pill have less chance of getting pregnant.

Main advantages: It's a highly effective method and convenient to use. Periods are more regular, with less cramps and less blood loss. There is less iron-deficiency anemia, less acne, less pelvic inflammatory disease, and fewer ectopic pregnancies among users. It may offer some protection from noncancerous breast tumors and ovarian cysts, as well as from ovarian and endometrial (lining of the uterus) cancer.

Who can use: Pill use is ruled out if you have, or have had, blood clots or inflammation in the veins, serious liver diseases, or unexplained bleeding from the vagina—also any suspicion of abnormal growth or cancer of the breast or uterus. You may need special tests to see whether you should take the pill if you have certain other conditions that could get worse using the pill, or a family history of certain diseases such as diabetes.

How this is used: The pill must be taken as directed. You're protected as long as you take them on time and don't skip any. If you see a doctor for some other reason, be sure to say you're on the pill. To get pregnant, stop the pills. Use another method until your periods become regular. Normal cycles usually return in a few months, but a few women may have trouble getting pregnant for a while after pill use.

---

* Careful and consistent use of methods can give better results than rates reported in actual use for average users. Schirm, A. L., et al. "Contraceptive Failure in the United States: The Impact of Social, Economic and Demographic Factors," *Family Planning Perspectives,* Vol. 14, No. 2, pp. 68, 1982.

After having a baby, get medical advice about when to go back on the pill, especially if nursing. Regular checkups are necessary while taking the pill.

Possible problems: Many women adjust with few or no problems. Pill users have a greater chance than nonusers of developing certain serious problems that may become fatal in rare cases, including blood clots, stroke, heart attack (to women age thirty-five and older), or liver tumors. Such chances increase with age and when certain other health problems are present. The risks are magnified by smoking more than fifteen cigarettes a day, by conditions such as high blood pressure, high levels of blood fat, or diabetes, or by being about 50 percent above ideal weight or thirty-five years of age or over. To learn more about possible problems with pill use, talk to your clinician and read the pill-package insert. Some minor reactions include breast tenderness, nausea, vomiting, weight gain or loss, and spotting between periods. These often clear up after two to three months of use. Combining the pill with other medicines such as antibiotics or drugs to control seizures may reduce the effectiveness of the pill in preventing pregnancy. Talk to your doctor about what to do. More detailed information about the risks of birth control pills and who should not use them is provided in the package insert that accompanies each package of birth control pills. It is essential that you read and understand this additional information.

Warning signals: Report immediately any of these signs: unusual swelling or pain in the legs; yellowing of skin or eyes; pain in the abdomen, chest, or arms; shortness of breath; severe headache; severe depression; or eye problems, such as blurred or double vision.

INTRAUTERINE DEVICE (IUD)

As of January 1986 the IUD may become very difficult to obtain in the United States because the major manufacturer has discontinued production. It is, however, still approved by the FDA for use.

What this is: A small device of plastic. (Some have copper or hormones.) A clinician inserts the right type in a woman's uterus. Some IUDs can be left indefinitely; other types must be renewed periodically.

What this does: An IUD acts to change the lining of the uterus in some way so that it hinders a pregnancy from happening.

How well this works*: Of one hundred women with IUDs, about five may become pregnant during the first year of actual use. Fewer pregnancies occur with continued use. A woman's protection is increased if she checks for the IUD string regularly, or if the couple also uses foam or condoms for a week about midway between periods.

Main advantages: With an IUD in place, a woman does not need to think about using her birth control method every day or every time she has sex.

Who can use: Certain conditions may rule out the use of IUDs. These include: certain abnormal conditions of the cervix, uterus, or ovaries; an active or recent infection of the tubes or ovaries; very heavy periods or abnormal bleeding from the vagina; presence of anemia; possible pregnancy; or history of previous tubal pregnancy. A history of heart disease needs special evaluation and care with insertion because of the chance of infection. Copper IUDs should not be used by women sensitive to copper or by women undergoing diathermy (heat) treatments.

How this is used: Insertion is often done during menstruation because the opening of the cervix is softer then. It may be somewhat painful, like bad menstrual cramps, but this is usually brief and goes away with a little rest and pain medication. A string on the IUD comes through the cervix into the vagina. You should feel for this now and then, especially after menstruation. It means the IUD is in place. You should have a checkup within three months, preferably soon after the first period following insertion. If pregnancy is desired, have the IUD removed by a clinician.

Possible problems: Most women adjust with few or no problems. But the following may occur: Cramping may be greater, mostly for a while after insertion. Bleeding may occur between periods. Periods may be heavier and may last longer. This occurs less with copper or hormone-releasing types. The IUD may fall out. If it's not noticed, pregnancy may result. Becoming pregnant while using an IUD is rare, but if signs of pregnancy occur, have a pelvic exam promptly. If you are pregnant, the device should be removed as soon as possible. This lessens the chance of serious infection that in rare cases might threaten life. It also reduces the chances of miscarriage or premature delivery. And if abortion is chosen, it should be done early. IUD users are at higher risk that an accidental pregnancy may be ectopic. If that happens, surgery is required. Infection of tubes or ovaries is not common, but it happens more often in IUD users than in nonusers. Women who have had pelvic infection before or who have had more than one sexual partner have greater chances of infection. Infection, with or without symptoms, may increase the risk of tubal pregnancy, cause sterility, or very rarely require removal of the reproductive organs. An infection that is not treated might become fatal. The use of copper IUDs may lessen the risk of infection, but they should not be used if a woman is allergic to copper or will undergo heat (diathermy) treatments. Rarely the IUD may puncture the wall of the uterus. If this happens, the IUD must be removed promptly by surgery.

Warning Signals: Report immediately any of these signs: severe cramping or increasing pain in the lower abdomen; pain during sex; unexplained fever and/or chills; increased or bad-smelling discharge; not being able to feel the string; a missed period or a late or light period.

THE CONDOM

What this is: A sheath of thin rubber or animal tissue. It is put on a man's erect penis before intercourse.

What this does: A condom collects a man's semen and keeps sperm from entering a woman's vagina.

How well this works*: For each one hundred couples relying on condoms, about ten pregnancies may occur during the first year of actual use. When the woman uses a vaginal contraceptive at the same time, there is greater protection.

Main advantages: Condoms are easy to get. They help protect against sexually transmissible diseases. They're a reliable and handy back-up or second method. They may help men with problems of premature ejaculation.

Who can use: Just about any man who wishes to can use a condom. Men with sensitivity to rubber may be rare exceptions. Condoms may be purchased by men and women, and there are no age restrictions.

How this is used: Either partner may roll a condom over the man's erect penis. About one-half inch at the tip is left slack to catch semen. After climax, but before losing the erection, hold the rim of the condom against the penis as the man withdraws. This way, the condom can't slip and spill semen. Then it's thrown away. A fresh one must be used for each act of intercourse.

Possible problems: Rough handling may tear rubber. Care is needed in withdrawing. Some couples object to it because it interrupts lovemaking. However, the man or woman can put the condom on as part of foreplay. Some users claim feeling is dulled.

Warning signals: None.

DIAPHRAGM

What this is: A soft rubber cup with a flexible ri: . around the edge. It's used with contraceptive cream or jelly.

What this does: It's inserted into a woman's vagina before intercourse. The diaphragm covers the entrance to the uterus, and the cream or jelly stops sperm.

How well this works*: Of one hundred women using diaphragms, about nineteen may become pregnant during the first year of actual use. You may increase protection by making sure that it covers the cervix following an insertion and before intercourse.

Main advantages: Once learned, insertion is easy. It can be part of bedtime routine or it can be shared by both partners during lovemaking. Properly placed, it is generally not felt by either the woman or the man.

Who can use: Diaphragm use is not recommended for women with poor muscle tone of the vagina, or those who have a sagging uterus or vaginal obstructions. Women not comfortable touching their genitals will probably not like the diaphragm.

How this is used: You must have the right size diaphragm prescribed for it to fit properly and work well. You will be shown how to put it in and take it out. Always use contraceptive cream or jelly with your diaphragm. It must be in place every time you have sex. Leave in place six to eight hours after last sexual intercourse. After a full-term pregnancy, or abortion or miscarriage beyond the first full three months of pregnancy, or pelvic surgery, or weight gain or loss of ten pounds or more, have the fit of your diaphragm checked.

Possible problems: Most women have no side effects. Some women who use a diaphragm are more prone to develop bladder infections. Occasional mild allergic reactions to rubber or cream or jelly may occur. Women with very short fingers may need to use an inserter. A diaphragm may become dislodged during sex if the woman is on top or has a relaxed vagina as a result of childbirth. Check the diaphragm for weak spots or pinholes from time to time by holding to the light.

Warning signals: Report promptly any discomfort when the diaphragm is in place or there is irritation or itching in the genital area, frequent bladder infections, or unusual discharge from the vagina.

VAGINAL CONTRACEPTIVE SPONGE

What this is: A soft, round-shaped sponge approximately two inches in diameter made of a synthetic substance impregnated with a spermicide. A nylon loop is attached across the bottom of the sponge for ease of removal.

What this does: The sponge is moistened and inserted into the vagina (much like a diaphragm) before intercourse. The "dimple" fits over the cervix. The sponge continuously releases a spermicide that halts sperm activity and acts as a barrier to block sperm from entering a woman's uterus.

How well this works*: Based on preliminary research of one hundred women using the sponge, nine to eleven will become pregnant. Pregnancy rates will likely be higher in actual use. Effectiveness can be further increased by using an additional method of contraception with the sponge, such as a condom.

Main advantages: It comes in one size. Once learned, insertion is easy. After insertion there's no need to wait to have sexual intercourse, and intercourse may be repeated within a twenty-four-hour period without additional preparation. There's little messiness or leakage. The spermicide contained in the sponge may offer some protection against certain sexually transmissible diseases. The sponge can be purchased without a prescription.

Who can use: Just about any woman who can use a tampon can use the sponge. However, a woman with short fingers may have difficulty placing and removing the sponge. Women not comfortable touching their genitals will probably not like the sponge.

How this is used: Hold the sponge in one hand with the "dimple" side facing the body. The loop should dangle under the sponge away from the body. Wet it with clean water (two tablespoons or more) so it's wet and drippy. Water activates the spermicide. Fold the sides of the sponge upward so the sponge looks long and narrow. Then slide the sponge through the opening of the vagina as far back in the vagina as your fingers will reach. When you let go of the sponge, it unfolds to cover the cervix. Check the position by sliding a finger around the edge of the sponge to make sure the cervix is covered. You should be able to feel the ribbon loop across the bottom of the sponge. It may be worn for up to twenty-four hours without change, but it must be left in place for six hours after the last act of intercourse prior to removal. Put a finger inside the vagina and hook it through the loop. Then slowly and gently pull the sponge out. The sponge is for one-time use only, and should never be reused. Always discard the old sponge in a waste container. Do not flush down the toilet. Do not use during menstruation. If you have any questions, any problems, or are unsure about how to use the sponge, you should consult with your physician or local family planning clinic.

Possible problems: Rarely, irritation may occur with use of the sponge due to an allergic reaction. If this happens, discontinuing use of the sponge should clear up the problem. Removal problems can occur. If the sponge cannot be removed, or if it fragments, a woman should call her physician or clinic for removal. There is some concern that sponge users may be at increased risk of toxic shock syndrome (TSS), which is associated with tampon use. Because the sponge is new, it is not known with certainty whether there is a definite relationship between TSS and sponge use. However, a few cases of TSS in which symptoms developed within twenty-four hours after sponge use have been reported. To minimize such a risk, do not leave the sponge in place longer than twenty-four hours, never use during menstruation, and avoid use after delivery of a baby or an abortion until your doctor approves. Some women complain of messiness.

Warning signals: Report promptly any itching or irritation in the genital area, persistent unpleasant odor or unusual discharge from the vagina.

VAGINAL CHEMICAL CONTRACEPTIVES

What this is: Foams, creams, jellies, and suppositories are chemical substances inserted deep into the vagina before intercourse that stop sperm but don't harm vaginal tissue.

What this does: A vaginal contraceptive inserted into a woman's vagina before intercourse spreads over the entrance to the uterus and blocks sperm from entering the uterus. The chemical stops sperm movement.

How well this works*: Of 100 women using a vaginal contraceptive, about eighteen may become pregnant during the first year of actual use. When the man uses a condom at the same time, greater protection is possible.

Main advantages: Easy to buy in drugstores. Easy to use. May offer some protection against certain sexually transmissible diseases.

Who can use: Almost any woman who wants to can use a vaginal contraceptive. Can be purchased by women and men; there are no age restrictions.

How this is used: Some are effective immediately; others require a ten-minute wait. Dosage quantities vary. Each product has directions on the package. Usually a woman lies down or squats and gently inserts the product deep into the vagina. Not effective for more than one hour after placement. More must be inserted if sex is repeated.

Possible problems: Not known to have bodily side effects. In rare cases a woman or man may find these products produce a slight genital irritation. Changing brands may help. If not used exactly as directed, these products may not form a good barrier to the uterus. Some women complain of messiness or leakage.

Warning signals: None.

FERTILITY AWARENESS WITH ABSTINENCE

What this is: Several ways of checking a woman's changing bodily signs to help her discover the days each month when an egg is likely to be released.

What this does: Knowing the several days before, during, and right after an egg is released lets a woman avoid unprotected intercourse during her peak fertility, to try to prevent live sperm from meeting the egg.

How well this works*: Among 100 women limiting intercourse by these methods, about twenty-four may become pregnant during the first year of actual use. Keeping careful records and consistent use can give better results.

Main advantages: No medication and little equipment are needed. Calendars, thermometers, and charts are easy to get. These methods are acceptable to all religious groups.

Who can use: A woman in good health who has been given careful instructions. Works best for women with regular menses. Most successful users combine taking their temperature each day and checking vaginal mucus.

How this is used: A woman's body temperature rises a little when an egg is released. Then it stays up until her next period. Her vaginal mucus increases just before an egg is released, and is clear and slippery. It reduces in quantity by four days after ovulation and becomes cloudy and sticky, and may disappear. Every day, temperature must be taken and/or vaginal mucus checked, and records kept. It is important to have individual instruction.

Possible problems: No bodily side effects to the user. Care is needed in keeping records and interpreting signs. Illness or even lack of sleep can produce false temperature signals. Vaginal infections or use of vaginal products or medication may alter changes in vaginal mucus.

Warning signals: None.

COMPARISON OF RISK OF DEATH FROM FERTILITY CONTROL METHODS*

Estimated annual number of deaths associated with pregnancy and childbirth resulting from failure to use a fertility control method and deaths associated with fertility control methods (including deaths occurring with pregnancy and childbirth when the contraceptive method fails) per 100,000 fertile sexually active women, by age group. Data based on U.S. Vital Statistics.

Method of Fertility Control Used	Woman's Age Group					
	15–19	20–24	25–29	30–34	35–39	40–44
No Method	7.0	7.4	9.1	14.8	25.7	28.2
The Pill Smokers Nonsmokers	2.4 0.5	3.6 0.7	6.8 1.1	13.7 2.1	51.4 14.1	117.6 32.0
IUD	1.3	1.1	1.3	1.3	1.9	2.1
Barrier Methods	3.0	2.8	1.9	1.5	2.5	3.2
Fertility Awareness with Abstinence	2.5	1.6	1.6	1.7	2.9	3.6
Abortion	0.5	1.1	1.3	1.9	1.8	1.1

* Howard W. Ory, "Mortality Associated with Fertility and Fertility Control," *Family Planning Perspectives,* 15 (March—April 1983), p. 60.

STERILIZATION

Methods of contraception intended to be permanent are the most effective means of controlling one's fertility. Sterilization is suitable only for those men and women who have decided they never want to cause conception or become pregnant. Information about surgical methods is available. If you're interested, ask your clinician for details.

Facts About STDs

ACQUIRED IMMUNE DEFICIENCY SYNDROME (called: AIDS)
18,576 cases reported by March 24, 1986.

Cause: Believed to be a virus.

First symptoms usually appear: Unknown—perhaps six months to five years after infection.

Symptoms may include: Profound fatigue, persistent fever, weight loss, painful lymph nodes, growths or lesions on skin, persistent diarrhea, thrush, unexplained bleeding.

Transmission: Spread through intimate contact with bodily fluids, usually blood or semen of infected person.

Diagnosis: White blood cell counts, skin testing, and antibody tests may help diagnose.

Treatment: No certain treatment for AIDS, though there are treatments for the "opportunistic" diseases which accompany it.

Complications: Fatal for AIDS, less so for ARC (AIDS Related Complex) or "lesser AIDS."

CHLAMYDIA

Cause: A parasite that is neither a virus nor bacteria.

First symptoms usually appear: May have no symptoms (70 percent of women).

Usual symptoms: Burning in urination, vaginal or urethral discharge, often occurs along with other venereal diseases.

Transmission: Sexual intercourse with infected partner.

Diagnosis: Culture, blood test for antibodies, microscopic test of secretions.

Treatment: The correct antibiotics, in the correct dosage; surgery in long-standing cases.

Complications:

MEN: Sterility.

WOMEN: Pelvic inflammatory disease; sterility.

NEWBORNS: Conjunctivitis; pneumonia; stillbirth; eye infections; blindness.

GONORRHEA (called: dose, clap, drip)   961,000 cases in 1982.

Cause: Bacterial.

First symptoms usually appear: Two to ten (up to thirty) days. 90 percent of infected women may have no symptoms.

Usual symptoms: White or yellow discharge from genitals or anus; pain on urination or defecation; pharyngeal (or throat) infections, usually symptomless.

WOMEN: Often no pain, or low abdominal pain, especially after menstrual periods.

MEN: 10 percent of infected men may have no symptoms.

Transmission: Direct contact of infected mucous membrane with the urethra, cervix, anus, throat, or eyes.

Diagnosis:

WOMEN: Culture.

MEN: Smear or culture.

Treatment: Series of antibiotics.

Complications:

WOMEN: Pelvic inflammatory disease (PID), sterility, arthritis; endocarditis, perihepatitis, meningitis.

MEN: Urethral stricture—erection problems; sterility; arthritis; endocarditis; perihepatitis; meningitis.

NEWBORNS: Blindness.

HERPES II (called: herpes)   20 million Americans are believed to suffer from herpes.

Cause: Viral.

First symptoms usually appear: Highly variable.

Usual symptoms: Cluster of tender, painful blisters in the genital area. Painful urination. Swollen glands, fever.

Transmission: Direct contact with blisters or open sores.

Diagnosis: Pap smear, culture taken when blisters or sores are present.

Treatment: Presently no cure. Treatment aims at relieving symptoms. May be linked with cervical cancer in women. A child may be infected during birth, resulting in severe central nervous system damage or death. So women with active herpes lesions should have their babies delivered by cesarean section.

MONILIAL VAGINITIS (called: moniliasis, vaginal thrush, yeast, candidiasis)

Cause: Fungal—frequently not caused by intercourse.

First symptoms usually appear: Varies.

Usual symptoms:

WOMEN: Thick, cheesy discharge, intense itching of genitals, skin irritation.

MEN: Usually no problem.

Transmission: The organism is frequently present in the mouth, vagina, and rectum without symptoms. Active symptoms may follow antibiotic therapy or direct contact with infected person.

Diagnosis: Microscopic identification.

Treatment: Prescription of creams, ointments, or suppositories; oral medication for resistant cases.

Complications:

WOMEN: Secondary infections by bacteria.

NEWBORNS: Mouth and throat infections.

NONGONOCOCCAL URETHRITIS (called NGU, SNU)

Cause: Chlamydia, bacteria.

First symptoms usually appear: One to three weeks.

Usual symptoms: Slight, white yellow or clear discharge from genitals, often only noticed in morning.

WOMEN: Usually no symptoms.

MEN: Mild discomfort from urination.

Transmission: Direct contact with infectious area.

Diagnosis: Smear or culture to rule out gonorrhea. Difficult to diagnose.

Treatment: Easily treated with oral antibiotics.

Complications:

> WOMEN: Pelvic inflammatory disease, sterility, eye infections, blindness.
>
> MEN: Sterility, prostate gland disorder, eye infections, blindness.
>
> NEWBORNS: Conjunctivitis, pneumonia, stillbirth.

PEDICULOSIS PUBIS (called: crabs, cooties)

Cause: Six-legged louse.

First symptoms usually appear: One to four weeks.

Usual symptoms: Intense itching, pinhead blood spots on underwear, nits in pubic hair.

Transmission: Direct contact with infested area or clothes/bedding containing nits or lice.

Diagnosis: Examination.

Treatment: Prescription or nonprescription drug applied to pubic area. Sexual partners must take treatment. Clothes/bedding must be washed or dry-cleaned.

Complication: Secondary infections as a result of scratching.

SCABIES (called: the itch)

Cause: Itch mite. Frequently not caused by intercourse.

First symptoms usually appear: Four to six weeks.

Usual symptoms: Severe itching at night, raised graying lines on skin where mites burrow—most frequently hands, genitals, breasts, stomach, buttocks.

Transmission: Direct contact with infested area or with clothes/bedding containing mites.

Diagnosis: Examination of affected areas.

Treatment: Nonprescription preparation applied to affected areas. Clothes/bedding must be washed or dry-cleaned.

Complications: Secondary infections as a result of scratching.

SYPHILIS: (called syph, pox, bad blood)   33,600 cases in 1982.

Cause: Spirochete.

First symptoms usually appear: Ten to ninety days (usually three weeks).

Usual symptoms:

> FIRST STAGE: Chancre (painless pimple, blister, or sore called chancre; pronounced "shanker") where spirochete entered body—genitals, anus, lips, breast, etc. Heals without treatment in one to five weeks.

> SECOND STAGE: Rash, mucous patches or condyloma warts (most are highly infectious), spotty hair loss, sore throat, swollen glands. Symptoms may reoccur for up to two years.

Transmission: Direct contact with infectious sores, rashes, or mucous patches.

Diagnosis: VDRL blood test or microscopic examination of organisms from sores.

Treatment: Long-acting penicillin or other antibiotics. Sexual partner must be treated at the same time.

Complications: Brain damage, insanity, paralysis, heart disease, death. Also damage to skin, bones, eyes, teeth, and liver of fetus and newborn children.

TRICHOMONIASIS (called trich, TV, Vaginitis)

Cause: Trichomonas vaginalis.

First symptoms usually appear: One to four weeks.

Usual symptoms:

> WOMEN: Heavy, frothy discharge; intense itching, burning, and redness of genitals.

> MEN: May have slight clear discharge from genitals and itching after urination. Usually no symptoms.

Transmission: Direct contact with infectious area.

Diagnosis: Pap smear, microscopic identification.

Treatment: Prescription drug taken by mouth.

Complication: Gland soreness and swelling.

VENEREAL WARTS (called: genital warts, condyloma acuminata)

Cause: Viral.

First symptoms usually appear: One to three months.

Usual symptoms: Local irritation, itching, wartlike growths, usually on the genitals or anus.

Transmission: Direct contact with warts.

Diagnosis: By examination.

Treatment: No specific cure. Warts may be removed by application of chemicals or surgically.

Complications: Highly contagious. Can spread enough to block vaginal, rectal, or throat openings. May predispose to cervical cancer in women.

Selected Bibliography for Parents and Children

BOOKS

For Children

GORDON, SOL and GORDON, JUDITH. *A Better Safe Than Sorry Book.* Fayetteville, NY: Ed-U Press, 1984.

GORDON, SOL and GORDON, JUDITH. Illustrated by Vivien Cohen. *Did the Sun Shine Before You Were Born?* Fayetteville, N.Y.: Ed-U Press, 1982.

NILSSON, LENNART. *How Was I Born? A Story in Pictures.* New York: Delacorte Press, 1975.

SHEFFIELD, MARGARET. *Where Do Babies Come From? A Book for Children and Their Parents.* New York: Alfred A. Knopf, 1973.

For Preteenagers

BETANCOURT, JEANNE. *Am I Normal?* New York: Avon Books, 1983.

———. *Dear Diary.* New York: Avon Books, 1983.

MADARAS, LYNDA with AREA MADARAS. *What's Happening to My Body?* New York: Newmarket Press, 1983.

MADARAS, LYNDA. *The "What's Happening to My Body?" Book for Boys.* New York: Newmarket Press, 1984.

For Teenagers

BAILIS, ANDREA. *What Are You Using? A Birth Control Guide for Teenagers.* New York: Dial Press, 1981.

CARRERA, MICHAEL. *Sex: The Facts, the Acts, and Your Feelings.* New York: Crown Publishers, 1981.

GORDON, SOL. *Facts About STD.* Fayetteville, N.Y.: Ed-U Press, 1983.

LIEBERMAN, E. JAMES and PECK, ELLEN. *Sex and Birth Control: A Guide for the Young.* New York: Harper & Row, 1981.

McCOY, KATHY. *The Teenage Body Book Guide to Sexuality.* New York: Simon & Schuster, 1983.

OETTINGER, KATHERINE B. with ELIZABETH C. MOONEY. *"Not My Daughter": Facing Up to Adolescent Pregnancy.* Englewood Cliffs, NJ: Prentice-Hall, 1979.

For Parents

ADAMS, CAREN and FAY, JENNIFER. *No More Secrets: Protecting Your Child from Assault.* San Luis Obispo, CA: Impact Publishers, 1981.

BELL, RUTH and WILDFLOWER, LENI ZEIGER. *Talking with Your Teenager: A Book for Parents.* New York: Random House, 1983.

CALDERONE, MARY S. and JOHNSON, ERIC W. Illustrated by Vivien Cohen. *The Family Book About Sexuality.* New York: Harper & Row, 1981.

——— and RAMEY, JAMES W. *Talking with Your Child About Sex.* New York: Random House, 1982.

GORDON, SOL and GORDON, JUDITH. *Raising a Child Conservatively in a Sexually Permissive World.* New York: Simon & Schuster, 1983.

LEWIS, HOWARD R. and LEWIS, MARTHA E. *Sex Education Begins at Home.* Norwalk, CT: Appleton-Century-Crofts, 1983.

USLANDER, ARLENE and WEISS, LEE DAVID. *Talking with Your Child About Sex.* Chicago: Budlong Press, 1978.

SUPPLEMENTARY LIST OF BOOKS, OUT OF PRINT BUT AVAILABLE IN LIBRARIES

Books for Children

GORDON, SOL. Illustrated by Vivien Cohen. *Girls Are Girls and Boys Are Boys: So What's the Difference?* 2nd ed. Fayetteville, NY: Ed-U Press, 1979.

Books for Preteenagers

HORVATH, JOAN. *What Girls Want to Know About Boys, What Boys Want to Know About Girls.* Nashville: Thomas Nelson Publishers, 1976.

Books for Parents

GORDON, SOL. *The Sexual Adolescent: Communicating With Teenagers About Sex.* 2nd ed. North Scituate, MA: Duxbury Press, 1979.

PAMPHLETS AND TEACHING RESOURCES

For Children

STRAIGHT TALK: SEXUALITY EDUCATION FOR PARENTS AND KIDS 4–7
MARILYN RATNER and SUSAN CHAMLIN. PP (Planned Parenthood) of Westchester, 88 East Post Road, White Plains, NY 10601, 1985. 48 pp. $4.95.

This resource for parents answers children's and their own questions about sex, roles, values, feelings, and appropriate behavior. It provides a foundation of basic knowledge as well as communication techniques and includes a pull-out activity section, *Kids' Place.*

WHY IS THAT LADY'S TUMMY SO BIG?
Choice, 1421 Arch, Philadelphia, PA 19102, 1981. $1.75.

This booklet is designed to help parents teach their young children about sexuality.

For Preteenagers:

GROWING OLDER: FACTS AND FEELINGS
JANE HIATT. Network Publications, 1700 Mission St., Santa Cruz, CA 95061-8506, 1983. $0.50.

This pamphlet describes body changes at puberty and the human reproductive system. Targeted for children in the fifth and sixth grades.

For Teens:

NOBODY TOLD ME IT WAS RAPE: A PARENTS' GUIDE FOR TALKING WITH TEENAGERS ABOUT ACQUAINTANCE RAPE AND SEXUAL EXPLOITATION
CAREN ADAMS and JENNIFER FAY. Network Publications, 1700 Mission, Santa Cruz, CA 95061-8506, 1984. 25 pp. $3.95.

A dynamic new resource designed to help parents educate and inform their adolescents about acquaintance rape; offers guidelines and skits to prevent sexual exploitation.

TALK TO ME ABOUT SEX, LOVE AND LIFE
BETH REIS and BARB McGUIRE. PP of Seattle-King County, 2211 East Madison, Seattle, WA 98112, 1983.

A series of booklets to improve communication between parents and children. Set up as a series of questions that can act as discussion starters. Available for parents, teens, and children, with separate booklets for different age groups and sexes. $2.50/set of two (one for parent, one for child).

For Parents:

HOW CAN I SAY IT?
ESTHER WALTER. PP of Mid-Iowa, Box 4557, Des Moines, IA 50306, 1982.
This booklet discusses how parents can talk to their children about sex. Comes with an accompanying booklet intended for teens. $1.00.

HOW TO TALK TO YOUR CHILD ABOUT SEX—A GUIDE FOR PARENTS
The National PTA, 700 N. Rush St., Chicago, IL 60611, 1985. 6 pp. $0.10 each.
An excellent booklet for parents with tips and techniques for talking with your child about sex. It includes a handy reading list.

LA FAMILIA ES IMPORTANTE (THE IMPORTANCE OF THE FAMILY)
PP of Orange County, 1801 N. Broadway, Santa Ana, CA 92706, 1984. 8 pp. $0.27 each.
This colorful, comic illustration booklet in Spanish is written in storybook form. It respects the boundaries of the Hispanic culture and demonstrates the importance of the family unit, stressing the values of family planning.

LET'S TALK ABOUT . . . S-E-X: A READ-AND-DISCUSS GUIDE FOR PEOPLE 9 TO 12 AND THEIR PARENTS.
SAM GITCHEL and LORRI FOSTER. PP of Fresno, 633 N. Van Ness, Fresno, CA 93728, 1983. 59 pp. $3.95.
This book is intended to help parents and their preadolescent sons or daughters develop better communication about sex. It includes factual information and brief activities which encourage dialogue about family values.

MY VERY OWN BOOK ABOUT ME
JO STOWELL and MARY DIETZEL. Lutheran Social Services of Washington, 1226 N. Howard, Spokane, WA 99201, 1980. $2.75.
A coloring activities book for children to help them learn about sexual abuse. Can also be used by parents to help discuss incidents of sexual abuse with their children.

NO MORE SECRETS
CAREN ADAMS and JENNIFER FAY. Impact Publishers, Box 1094, San Luis
   Obispo, CA 93406, 1981. $3.95.
   A booklet for parents about how to teach their children to
   avoid sexual abuse.

OH NO! WHAT DO I DO NOW?
SIECUS, 80 Fifth Avenue, New York, NY 10011, 1983. $1.50.
   Details difficult situations that may arise in dealing with chil-
   dren's sexuality, and how to cope with them. Also available in
   Spanish.

OUR CHILDREN'S SELF-ESTEEM
MARY NELSON. Network Publications, 1700 Mission St., Santa Cruz, CA
   95061-8506, 1983. $0.25 each.
   This brochure discusses the importance of instilling a strong
   sense of self-esteem in our children.

*PARENTS TALK LOVE: THE CATHOLIC HANDBOOK ABOUT
SEXUALITY*
SUSAN K. SULLIVAN and MATTHEW A. KAWIAK. Paulist Press, 997 Mac-
   Arthur Blvd., Mahwah, N.J. 07430, 1985. 164 pp. $7.95
   This sensitive book, written by a Catholic priest and experi-
   enced sexuality educator, helps parents accept the responsibility
   for the sexual education of their children.

SEX ON TV: A GUIDE FOR PARENTS
DAVID LLOYD GREEN. Network Publications, 1700 Mission St., Santa
   Cruz, CA 95061-8506, 1982. $1.95.
   This booklet provides practical, nonthreatening examples of
   how television can be used as a positive springboard for parent-
   child communication. Shows how television influences sexual attitudes and stereotypes.

*TALKING TO CHILDREN/TALKING TO PARENTS ABOUT SEX-
UAL ASSAULT*
LOIS LOONTJENS. Network Publications, 1700 Mission St., Santa Cruz,
   CA 95061-8506, 1984. 68 pp. $10.95.
   Based on the PBS television series, "Child Sexual Abuse: What
   Your Children Should Know," this guide provides presentations
   on sexual assault to children and parents.

*THE PARENT'S HANDBOOK/STEP: SYSTEMATIC TRAINING
FOR EFFECTIVE PARENTING*
DON DINKMEYER and GARY D. MCKAY. American Guidance Service,
Circle Pines, MN 55014, 1982. 121 pp. $6.95.

STEP provides a practical approach to parent-child relations.
This handbook is the guide to a democratic philosophy of child
training. There is a companion book available, as well as several
pamphlets on effective parenting skills.

THE SATURDAY NOTEBOOK
THOMAS MOORE et al. The East Woods Press, 429 East Blvd., Charlotte,
NC 28203, 1983. $8.95.

An activity workbook that parents and children can share. A
page for the adult facing a page for the child allows both to write
and draw their thoughts at the same time.

THE WHOLE CHILD: A SOURCEBOOK
STEVANNE AUERBACH, Ph.D. G. P. Putnam's Sons, 1981. 304 pp. $8.95.

A comprehensive, easy-to-use sourcebook which reviews, ana-
lyzes, and condenses the knowledge of the experts on every
phase of child care from conception through school age.

WHAT EVERYONE SHOULD KNOW ABOUT AIDS
Scriptographic Booklets. Channing L. Bete Co., Inc., 200 State Rd., S.
Deerfield, MA 01373, 1983. $0.39 each.

Written in the simple "pictographic" style, this booklet explains
the basic facts about AIDS and current research into the cause
and possible cure for the disease. A Spanish version is also available.

Index

Abnormalities, questions about, 54–55

Abortion, 114, 121–24, 166–67
  comparative risk, 180
  and IUDs, 174

Abstinence, 155
  with fertility awareness methods, 179–80

Abuse, sexual, of children, 22
  protection from, 125–37
  rape, 133–37

Abused child, help for, 131–33

Acceptance, in adolescence, 35

Acne, and "the pill," 171

Acquired immune deficiency syndrome. *See* AIDS

"Acting out," sexual, 145

Activities, during menstruation, 66–67

Adolescence, 56–60, 155–56, 167
  and parenthood, 120–21
  See also Puberty

Adolescents
  latchkey children, 146–50
  need for acceptance, 35
  need for sex information, 22–23
  pregnancies of, 3
  reasons to avoid intercourse, 60, 104–5
  self-esteem of, 33–36
  sexually active, 83
  in single-parent families, 140–41, 143–45
  See also Puberty; Teenagers

Adoption, 114, 118

Advertising, sexuality in, 3
  and grade school children, 52–53

Affection, learning of, 16

After-school programs, 148–49

Age
  and "the pill," 172
  for pregnancy, 81
  for sex activity, 97–99
  of sexual maturity, 8–9
  for teaching birth control, 82

AIDS, 88–89, 182

AIDS related complex (ARC), 182

Alan Guttmacher Institute study, 86

Alcohol, and rape, 135

Amenorrhea, 67

Anemia
  and IUDs, 173
  and "the pill," 171

Animal behavior, small child and, 17–18

Anorexia, 67

Antibiotics, and "the pill," 172

ARC (AIDS related complex), 182

Asymptomatic STDs, 88

Attitudes to sexuality, 7–8

Babies, source of
    child's idea of, 40–42
    preschool questions, 51
Baby-sitters, and sexual abuse, 129
Barrier contraceptives, 84
    comparative risk, 180
    See also Condoms; Diaphragms;
        Sponges, contraceptive
Barthalow-Koch, Patricia, 41
Basal body temperature monitoring,
    84
    See also Fertility awareness
        methods of birth control
Bernstein, Anne C., 40–41, 42
Bibliography, 188–95
Birth
    child's idea of, 17, 40–42
    grade school questions, 54–55
    preschool questions, 51
Birth control
    methods, 170–81
        comparative risks, 180
        questions about, 81–87
        and sexually transmissible
            diseases, 90
    responsibility for, 102–3
Black children, adoption of, 118
Bladder infections, and diaphragms,
    176
Blood clots, and "the pill," 171, 172
Blood fat levels, and "the pill," 172
Blood loss, in menstruation, 65
Blood test, to establish paternity, 117
Body odor, at puberty, 156
Body parts
    naming of, 17, 40, 49
    and sexual abuse, 129
    preschool curiosity, 49–50
Books, helpful
    for children, 17, 188–90
    for parents, 189, 190
    for preteenagers, 188–89, 190
    for teenagers, 189, 190
Boys
    as baby-sitters, 129
    child molestation, 125
    without fathers, 13–14
    hormonal changes, 64, 155–56
    information about menstruation,
        64
    pubertal changes, 57–58

self-esteem, and sexual behavior,
    34
sex information needs, 79
sexuality education for, 19–21
sexual maturity of, 69–72
views of sex, 99–100
Breasts, 156
    enlargement in boys, 72
    preschool questions, 50–51
Briggs, Dorothy, 36

Calendar rhythm, 84
Cancer
    and herpes, 184
    and "the pill," 171
    and venereal warts, 187
Candidiasis, 184
Cervical cancer
    and herpes, 184
    and venereal warts, 187
Cervical mucous examination, 84–85
    See also Fertility awareness
        methods of birth control
Cervix, 155, 156, 168
Chemical contraceptives, 178–79
Childbirth, 156
    and herpes infection, 184
    See also Newborns
Child care centers, and sexual
    abuse, 129–30
Child molestation, 126
    See also Sexual abuse of children
Children
    with AIDS, 88
    helpful books for, 188–90
    pamphlets and teaching resources,
        190–91
    questions of, 25
    sexual abuse of, 22, 125–31
    sexuality of, 8
    sexually abused, help for, 131–33
    in single-parent families, 141–45
Children's books, sexuality taught
    by, 17
Child support, and paternity, 117
Chlamydia, 87, 88, 90, 182–83
Cigarette smoking, and "the pill,"
    172, 180
Circumcision, 156–57
Climax, 157, 161, 168
    male, 158
Clitoris, 157, 160

Communication, parent-child, 5, 6,
    24–25, 54, 94–96, 101
  difficulties of, 9–10
  protection from sexual abuse, 131
  in single-parent families, 145
  with teenagers, 110–11
Conception, 157
Condoms, 84–85, 157–58, 165, 174–75
  and chemical contraceptives, 178
  and contraceptive foam, 160
  and IUDs, 173
  and sexually transmissible
    diseases, 89, 90
Condyloma acuminata, 186–87
Contraception, 157–58, 170–81
  withdrawal, 168–69
Contraceptives, 81–87, 110–11, 168
  oral, 163–64
  risks of, 123
  and sexually transmissible
    diseases, 87, 89, 90
Conversation openers for older
    child, 18
Cooties. See Pediculosis pubis
Copper IUDs, 173, 174
Costs of abortions, 123
Counsel
  for pregnant teenagers, 113
  for rape victims, 136
  in unintended pregnancies, 113,
    121
Crabs. See Pediculosis pubis
Cramps
  after IUD insertion, 173
  menstrual, 66
Creams, contraceptive, 158, 168, 176,
    178
Crushes, teenage, 92, 161
Curiosity about sex
  of preschoolers, 51
  among teenagers, 77

D&E (dilation and evacuation), 122
Date rape, 133–35
Daughters, and fathers, 13
Decision-making, and self-esteem, 34
Decisions, in unintended pregnancy,
    114–16
Developmental stages, 38–44
  early grade school (ages six to
    nine), 51–56
  preschool, 49–51

preteen years (ages nine to
    twelve), 56–60
Diabetes, and "the pill," 172
Diaphragms, 84–85, 158, 175–76
  and sexually transmissible
    diseases, 89
Diathermy, and IUDs, 173, 174
Dilation and evacuation (D&E), 122
Diseases, sexually transmitted. See
    Sexually transmissible
    diseases
Divorce
  children of, 142–44
  and teenage marriages, 4, 117

Economic situation, and teenage
    pregnancy, 118, 120
Ectopic pregnancies
  and IUDs, 174
  and "the pill," 171
Education
  and teenage pregnancy, 118, 120
  of unmarried mothers, 4
Egg cells, 157, 159, 160, 162, 164, 166
  maturing, diagram, 62–63
Ejaculation, 57, 69, 156, 158, 159, 163,
    164, 166, 168
Elementary school child. See Grade
    school years
Emotional expr ssion, learning of, 16
Emotional maturity, and early sexual
    experiences, 60
Epididymus, diagram, 70
Erections, 69, 156–59, 163
  involuntary, 71
Estrogen, 162
Ethnic differences in adoption
    choice, 118
Exploitation, in early sex relations,
    60

Fallopian tubes, 155–57, 159, 160, 162,
    164
  diagram, 62–63
False statements about birth control,
    84
FAM. See Fertility awareness
    methods
Family, child sexual abuse in, 126
Family albums, 17
Family roles, 12
Fantasies, sexual, 96–97, 156

Fathers
  and adoption choice, 119
  family roles, 12–13
  sex discrimination among
    children, 13
Fear
  of adults, as symptom of sexual
    abuse, 132
  of sex, among teenagers, 77
Female hormones, 162
Female sex organs, 160
Fertility, 162
  after menopause, 162
Fertility awareness methods (FAM)
    of birth control, 84, 158, 159–
    60, 162–63
  with abstinence, 179–80
  comparative risks, 180
Fertilization, 157, 160, 166
Foam, contraceptive, 158, 160, 168,
    178
  and condoms, 158
  and IUDs, 173
Foreskin, 156–57
Freud, Anna, 43
Freud, Sigmund, 38, 51

Gagnon, John, 96
Gale, Jay, 19
Gay. See Homosexuality
Gender awareness of preschool
    child, 49
Gender identity, development of, 16,
    38–39
Gender-related roles
  in families, 13
  taught to small child, 17
Gender-related views of sex, 99–100
Genital herpes, 88, 156, 183–84
Genitals, 160
  development of, 57–58
  discharge from, 165
  naming of, 40
  and sexually transmissible
    diseases, 89
  symptoms of sexual abuse, 132
Genital warts, 186–87
Girls
  child molestation, 125
  without fathers, 13–14
  hormonal changes, 64, 155
  masturbation of, 75–76

pubertal changes, 57–58
self-esteem, and sexual behavior,
    34
sex information needs, 78
sexual excitation, 156, 157
sexually active, in single-parent
    families, 144–45
teenage, as parents, 120–21
views of sex, 99–100
Gonorrhea, 87, 88, 90, 165, 183
Goodman, Ellen, 31
Grade school years (ages six to
    nine), 51–56
Growth patterns in puberty, 69
Guilt feelings
  and birth control, 82
  early development of, 38
  from masturbation 74, 75

Health, during pregnancy, 120
Heart attack, and "the pill," 172
Heart disease, and IUDs, 173
Heat treatments, and copper IUDs,
    173, 174
Herpes, 89, 165, 183–84
Heterosexual, 160
High blood pressure, and "the pill,"
    172
Home, sexuality learned at, 3–5
Homosexuality, 90–93, 160–61
  and masturbation, 75
Hormone-releasing IUDs, 173
Hormones, 161
  changes caused by, 58, 64, 155–56
  female, 162
  male, 167
Hygiene
  during menstrual period, 69
  and sexually transmissible
    diseases, 90, 165
Hymen, 99
  and masturbation, 76

Ignorance, and birth control, 83
Illness, and menstrual irregularity,
    67
Impersonal conversations about
    sexual matters, 32
Incest, 126
  between latchkey children, 147
Induced abortion, 166–67
Infants, sexuality of, 37–38

Infatuation, 105–6
Intercourse, 163, 164, 165
    climax, 157
    contraceptives, 168
    first experiences, 78, 99
    questions about, 77–81
        preschool questions, 51
    withdrawal, 168–69
    young child's idea of, 49–50
    for young people, reasons to
        avoid, 60, 104–5
Interpersonal relations, and
    sexuality education, 11–12
IntraUterine Device. See IUD
"Itch," 185
IUD (IntraUterine Device), 84–85,
    158, 161, 170, 172–74
    comparative risk, 180

Jellies, contraceptive, 158, 168, 176,
    178

Kelley, Joan, 143–44

Labia, 161, 168
Latchkey children, 146–50
Latency phase, Freudian, 51–52
Latino children, adoption of, 118
Legal considerations in abortion, 122
Lice. See Pediculosis pubis
Listening, by parents, 26–28
Liver disease, and "the pill," 171, 172
Love
    and infatuation, 105–6
    and sex, 81

Magical thinking
    about birth control, 82, 83
    about pregnancy, 79
Male hormones, 167
Male sex organs, 160
Marriage, 117–18
    of teenagers, divorce, 4
Masculinity
    and sexuality, 12
    stereotypical, 71
Masturbation, 73–76, 157, 161
    by small children, 43
Maturity
    and sex relationships, 98–99
    and sexual activity, 104–5
Media, and sexuality, 3, 52–53

See also Television
Medicaid, for abortions, 123
Medications, and "the pill," 172
Menopause, 161–62
Menstruation, 57, 61–68, 155, 156,
    162, 167
    preteen information, 56
    questions about, 47–48
Miscarriage, 166, 167
Misinformation
    about birth control, 83, 84
    problems of, 23
    about sexuality, 9
Monilial vaginitis, 184
Moniliasis, 184
Motherhood, unrealistic ideas of, 121
Mothers, sexuality education from,
    12
Mucus/Temperature Method, 159–60,
    179–80
    See also Fertility awareness
        methods of birth control
Music, popular, sexuality of, 3

Natural Family Planning, 159
Netherlands, teen pregnancy rates,
    86
Newborns
    and chlamydia, 183
    and gonorrhea, 183
    and herpes, 184
    and monilial vaginitis, 184
    and nongonococcal urethritis, 185
    and syphilis, 186
NGU. See Nongonococcal urethritis
Nightmares, as symptom of sexual
    abuse, 132
Nocturnal emissions, 56, 59, 69–71
Nongonococcal urethritis (NGU,
    SNU), 184–85
Normality
    preoccupation with
        of grade school children, 55
        of preteen years, 57
        of pubertal boys, 71–72
        of teenagers, 35
    of sexual thoughts, 96–97

Oral contraceptives, 163–64
Oral sex, 103
    and sexually transmissible
        diseases, 89

Orgasm, 157
Out-of-wedlock birth, 117
Ovarian cysts, and "the pill," 171
Ovaries, 155, 162
    diagram, 62–63
    in menopause, 161–62
Overweight, and "the pill," 172
Ovulation, 67, 162–63
    diagram, 62–63
Ovulation Method, 159–60
Ovum, 163
    See also Egg cells

Pamphlets, 190–94
Parental consent
    for abortion of minor, 122
    not needed for STD treatment, 89,
        166
Parenthood
    in adolescence, 120–21
    responsibilities of, 79–80
Parents
    communication with children, 5, 6
        difficulties of, 9–10
    helpful books for, 189, 190
    pamphlets and teaching resources,
        192–94
    and pregnancy of daughter, 112–13
    questions from children, 24–26
    and self-esteem of children, 35–36
    sex education of, 7–8
    and sexual activity of child, 109–
        11
    sexuality education from, 5, 21–23
    unmarried, sexual relationships of,
        138–45
    working, and latchkey children,
        146–50
Paternity
    and adoption choice, 119
    responsibilities of, 116–17
Pediculosis pubis, 185
Peer pressure for sexual activity, 20,
    101–2
Pelvic infections, and IUDs, 174
Pelvic inflammatory disease (PID),
    88
    and "the pill," 171
Penis, 155, 157, 160, 163–65, 167
    circumcision, 156–57
    diagram, 70
    erection, 158–59

growth of, 57
preschool questions, 50
sexually transmissible disease
    symptoms, 89
size of, 72
Periods, 65, 162, 163
    and IUDs, 173
    with "the pill," 171
    See also Menstruation
Personality changes, as symptom of
    sexual abuse, 132
Pharyngeal gonorrhea, 89
Piaget, Jean, 37, 38
Picture albums, 17
Pictures, drawn by small child, 17
PID (pelvic inflammatory disease),
    88, 171
"The Pill," 84–85, 158, 163–64, 170–72
    comparative risk of, 180
Planned Parenthood
    and adoption, 119
    literature from, 16
    public opinion survey, 11, 110, 151
Planned Parenthood centers
    for birth control information, 84
    information about sexually
        transmissible diseases, 89
    for information of pregnancy, 80
    for prenatal care information, 120
    for rape counseling, 136
"Playing doctor," 39, 49
Pleasure, from sex, 99
PMS (premenstrual syndrome), 66–67
Praise, and self-esteem, 34–35
Pregnancy, 156, 157, 164, 165
    before menstruation, 67
    child's idea of, 40–42
    contraception, 158, 168
    fear of, 79
    and IUDs, 173–74
    and menstruation, 68, 162
    questions about, 77–81
        grade school questions, 54–55
        preschool questions, 50–51
    risks for young people, 60
    small child and, 17
    of teenagers, 3, 86
    termination of, 166–67. See also
        Abortion
    tests for, 113
Premature ejaculation, and condoms,
    174

Premenstrual syndrome (PMS), 66–67
Prenatal care, 120
Prepuberty
    sex education, 77–78
    sexual interests, 43
Preschool child, 49–51
    sexual behavior of, 39
    See also, Young child
Preschools, and sexual abuse, 129–30
Preteen years (ages nine to twelve),
    56–60
    helpful books for, 188–89, 190
    pamphlets and teaching resources,
    191
Privacy, needed by child, 29–32
Progesterone, 162
Prostate gland, 164
    diagram, 70
Psychosexual development of child,
    37–44
Puberty, 56–59, 155–56, 159, 161, 164
    changes of, 35, 43
        female, 168
        male, 69–72
    grade school questions, 55–56
    ovarian function, 162
    parent-child relationships, 78
    See also Adolescence
Pubic area, 164
Pubic hair, 57–58, 156, 168

Questions
    by grade school children (ages six
        to nine), 53–56
    about masturbation, 75–76
    by preschoolers, 50–51
    by preteens, 58–60
    by teenagers, 61–93
        parents' answers, 24–26

Rape, 133–37
Refusal of sex, tactful, 100–1
Relationships, and sex, 97
Reproduction
    child's understanding of, 40–42
    grade school questions, 54–55
    preschool questions, 51
Reproductive organs, 62–64
Reproductive system, 155–56
Responsibilities
    of parenthood, 79–80

for prevention of pregnancy, 83–
    84, 102–3
Rhythm Method, 159–60
Risks
    of abortion, 122–23
    comparative, of birth control
        methods, 180
    of contraceptives, 123
    in sexual relationship, 100
Roles, parental, 12
Romances, teenage, 105–6
Runaways, and sexual abuse, 126

Sanitary pads, 65–66
Saying no, 100–1
Scabies, 185
Schools
    and sexuality education, 4, 10
    and teenage pregnancy, 120
Scrotum, 155, 160, 164, 167
    diagram, 70
Self-esteem
    development of, 33–36
    and rape, 134–36
    and sexuality education, 11
Semen, 157, 158, 164–166
Seminal vesicles, 165
    diagram, 70
Sex education, 11
    lack of, 9
    of latchkey children, 148
    from others than parents, 77–78
    from parents, 151
    in schools, 4, 10
    sources of, 43–44
    in Sweden, 41–42
Sex hormones, 58, 64, 161
Sex organs, external, 160
Sex role stereotyping, 71, 99–100
    and rape, 133–34
    and sexual identity, 91
Sexual abuse of children, 22
    of latchkey children, 147
    protection from, 125–37
Sexual behavior of adolescents
    and self-esteem, 33–34, 36
    study of, 86
Sexual identity
    development of, 43
    questions of, 90–93
Sexual intercourse. *See* Intercourse
Sexuality

defined, 4–5
development of, 37–44
Sexually transmissible diseases
  (STDs), 4, 60, 87–90, 165, 182–
  87
  and chemical contraceptives, 178
  and condoms, 174
  and contraceptive sponges, 177
  and oral sex, 103
Sexual maturity, age of, 8–9
Siamese twins, origin of, 55
Single-parent families, 13–14
Single parenthood, 138–45
Sleep disturbances, as symptom of
  sexual abuse, 132
Small child, sex education of, 15–19
Smoking, and "the pill," 172, 180
SNU. See Nongonococcal urethritis
Social behavior, discussion of, 18
Songs, popular, sexuality of, 3
Sore throat, 89
Sperm cells, 155, 157–60, 162, 164–68
  and masturbation, 161
Spermicides, 84
Sponges, contraceptive, 84–85, 176–
  78
Spontaneous abortion, 166, 167
Sports, during menstruation, 66–67
STDs. See Sexually transmissible
  diseases
Stereotypical sex roles, 91, 97, 99–
  100
  birth control, 102–3
Sterilization, 166, 181
Straight. See Heterosexual
Stroke, and "the pill," 172
Suppositories, contraceptive, 158,
  168, 178
Survey of Family Growth, 82
Sweden
  sex education in, 41–42
  teen pregnancy rates, 86
Symptoms
  of AIDS, 182
  of chlamydia, 182
  of gonorrhea, 183
  of herpes, 184
  of monilial vaginitis, 184
  of nongonococcal urethritis, 184
  of pediculosis pubis, 185
  of pregnancy, 80
  of rape, 136

of scabies, 185
of sexual abuse, 132–33
of sexually transmissible diseases,
  89, 165
  lacking, 88
of syphilis, 186
of trichomoniasis, 186
of venereal warts, 186
warning signals
  with contraceptive sponges, 178
  with diaphragm use, 176
  with IUD use, 174
  when using "the pill," 172
Sympto-Thermal Method, 159–60
  See also Fertility awareness
  methods of birth control
Syphilis, 89, 165, 185–86

Tampons, 65–66
Teaching resources, 190–94
Teasing, 96
Teenagers
  with AIDS, 88
  and birth control, 82
  early sexual experience, 99
  frequency of intercourse, 83
  helpful books for, 189, 190
  information needs of, 11–12, 22–23,
    110
  intercourse experiences, 78
    reasons to avoid, 60, 104–5
  marriages, 117–18
  pamphlets and teaching resources,
    191
  as parents, 120–21
  pregnancies of, 3, 112–24
    reduction of, 151
    study of, 86
  privacy needed by, 29–32
  questions of, 24–26, 61–93
  responsibility of, 104–5
  self-esteem of, 33–36
  and sexually transmissible
    diseases, 87–90
  See also Adolescents; Puberty
Television, sexual material on, 21,
  22, 81
  and grade school children, 52–53
  and sexuality, 147–48
  and small children, 18
Temperature checks, determining
  fertility by, 179–80

Termination of pregnancy, 166–67
    See also Abortion
Testicles, 155, 160, 164, 166, 167
    diagram, 70
Testosterone, 69, 167
Tests for pregnancy, 113
Thrush, vaginal, 184
Toilet training, and sexual
    perceptions, 38–39
Toxic shock syndrome, 66
    and contraceptive sponges, 177–78
Trichomoniasis, 186
Trust, between parents and
    teenagers, 32, 96
Tubal pregnancy, and IUDs, 173, 174
TV. *See* Trichomoniasis

Underarm hair, 57, 58
Unintended pregnancies, 3, 82–87,
    112–24
    reduction of, 151
United States, teenage sexual
    behavior, 86
Unmarried fathers, legal rights of,
    119
Unmarried mothers, 138–45
    education of, 4
Urethra, 157, 167
    diagram, 70
Urination
    and ejaculation, 158, 163
    after intercourse, and sexually
        transmissible diseases, 89
    painful, 165, 167
    preschool questions, 50
Urine, abnormal, 89
Uterus, 155–58, 160, 164, 166, 167
    diagram, 62–63

Vacuum aspiration, 122
Vagina, 155, 156, 158, 160, 163, 165–68
    sexually excited, 156, 157
Vaginal bleeding
    after IUD insertion, 173
    unexplained, and "the pill," 171
Vaginal contraceptives, 158, 168

chemical contraceptives, 178–79
    and condoms, 174
    foam, 160
    and sexually transmissible
        diseases, 89, 165
    sponges, 176–78
Vaginal discharges, 89
Vaginal thrush, 184
Vaginitis. *See* Trichomoniasis
Values
    learning of, 143
    of self. *See* Self-esteem
    and sexual relations, 94–106
Vas deferens, 168
VD. *See* Sexually transmissible
    diseases
Venereal disease. *See* Sexually
    transmissible diseases
Venereal warts, 186–87
Virgin
    first intercourse, 78, 99
    pregnant, 80
Virginity, questions about, 75, 76
Voice changes, 57, 58
Vulva, 160, 168

Wallerstein, Judith, 143–44
Wall Street Journal survey, 52–53
Washing of genitals, and sexually
    transmissible diseases, 165
Wet dreams, 69–70, 168
    See also Nocturnal emissions
Withdrawal, 84, 168–69
Womb. *See* Uterus

Yeast (monilial vaginitis), 184
Young child
    privacy needed by, 30
    sex education of, 15–19
    sexual development, 38–40
    sexuality of, masturbation, 73
    See also Preschool child; Preteen
        years
Young people, reasons to avoid
    intercourse, 60, 104–5